100 YEARS OF THE WIMBLEDON
TENNIS CHAMPIONSHIPS
James Medlycott

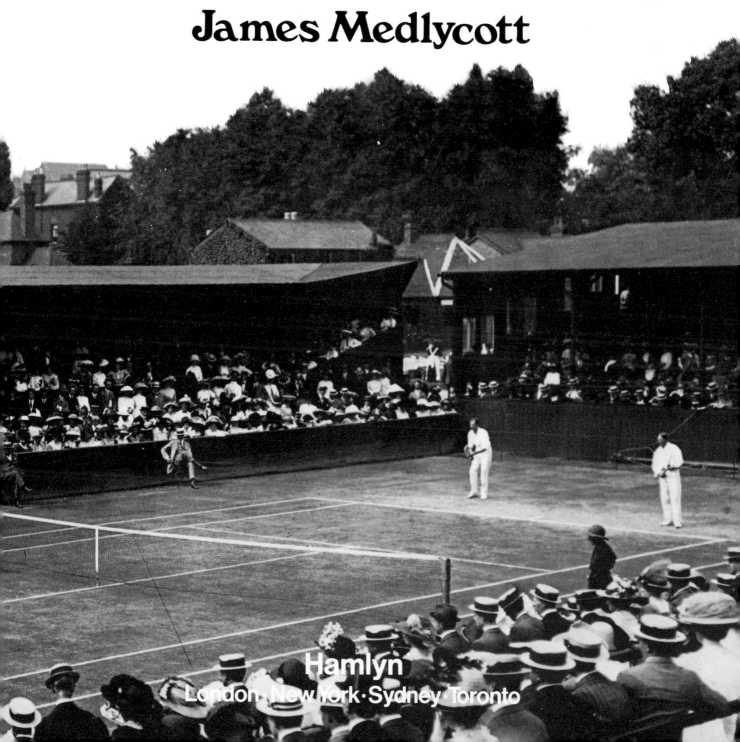

Hamlyn
London · New York · Sydney · Toronto

The pictures on the preliminary pages and endpapers are as follows:
Front endpaper Wimbledon during the 1923 championships. Court No. 2 doesn't look much different today.
Title page Men's doubles at the old Wimbledon, Worple Road, in 1911. A.F. Wilding is receiving service and M.J.G. Ritchie is back on the baseline. This 'old-fashioned' formation is still used by John Newcombe and Tony Roche today.
Facing foreword page Rain never intimidates Wimbledon aficionados, and if you are not properly equipped you can always improvise.

Foreword page J. Donald Budge, arguably the greatest player in the history of the game. He won all three events in both 1937 and 1938, the men's doubles with C. Gene Mako. They celebrate the hundredth meeting by pairing up once more for the veterans' doubles.
Back endpaper Wimbledon in the 1920s, looking very much as it does in the 1970s.

The front cover pictures are of Chris Evert and Björn Borg, with, inset, G.L. Patterson and Mrs Lambert Chambers. The back cover picture is of Courts No. 4 & 5.

Published by The Hamlyn Publishing Group Limited
London · New York · Sydney · Toronto
Astronaut House, Feltham, Middlesex, England

Filmset by Filmtype Services Limited, Scarborough, England
Printed by Cox and Wyman Ltd, Fakenham, England

Contents

Foreword

Forty-one years ago I achieved my greatest ambition by winning the Wimbledon singles championship – and the men's and mixed doubles for good measure.

Without the slightest reservation, that year remains the highspot of my career, along with a Davis Cup victory over my much admired friend, the late Gottfried von Cramm, on the Centre Court.

Now, when I return each year to strive for the veterans' doubles title, the thrill of walking through the famous Doherty gates and up the broad walk to the main club-house is every bit as strong as it was then.

I am not alone in feeling that way about Wimbledon. My constant contact with the front-runners of today confirms my belief that these remain the greatest championships of all and the singles the title players cherish above all others.

One other special facet differentiates Wimbledon from the rest of the circuit. Each year the focal point of all tennis-playing nations and the host to their players and ILTF representatives, Wimbledon is an unequalled maker of new friendships.

It was forty-two years ago that I met Jim, the author of this book, on the first afternoon of the first tournament in which I played. Wimbledon cemented a friendship which has lasted ever since. I have come to respect his judgment of the game and can think of no man better suited to the writing of a perceptive review of the 100 years of the Wimbledon championships.

J. Donald Budge

The Wimbledon Story

Beginnings: 1877-1914

Two hundred enthusiasts watched Spencer Gore beat W.C. Marshall 6-1, 6-2, 6-4 to become the first Wimbledon champion back in July 1877. Who among that meagre number could have foreseen that 100 years later the total audience would run into tens, hundreds maybe, of millions: 15,000 around the eternal Centre Court and the balance via television and radio, media undreamt of in those leisurely days?

Certainly not Gore himself. In his own assessment of the game, it was 'extremely doubtful' that anyone 'who has really played well at cricket, tennis (the old game of Kings), or even rackets, will ever seriously give his attention to lawn tennis, beyond showing himself to be a promising player.'

Björn Borg, Jimmy Connors, Arthur Ashe, Billie Jean King, and Chris Evert are but five of the lawn tennis – henceforth 'tennis' – millionaires who have proved him wrong. And scattered around the world 50 million or more active devotees owe much of their athletic happiness to Major Walter Clopton Wingfield, to whom the invention of the game is usually attributed, and to those Wimbledon visionaries, J.H. Walsh, Julian Marshall, Henry Jones, and C.G. Heathcote, who conceived, campaigned for, and eventually administered the first championship, so kindling a spark that began the blaze which was to spread throughout the world.

Not that this was their main intention. Maybe those were leisurely days for the middle and upper classes but even a prestige organization like the All England Croquet and Lawn Tennis Club knew something of the economic pinches which have, like Wimbledon, persisted for the past 100 years. The club needed a new roller to maintain its lawns in the immaculate state which had first suggested to the enthusiasts their splendid suitability for the new game spreading across the country. So the proposal to stage a money-raising tournament was accepted, a cup costing 25 guineas was provided by *The Field* magazine, of which Mr Walsh was editor, and twenty-two eager men replied to the advertisement in *The Times* inviting entries. Gore, then twenty-seven years old, took the title though the final was delayed from 12 to 16 July because the annual Eton v

1
Major Walter Clopton Wingfield. He started the tennis craze when he patented the game 'Sphairistike' in 1874. All but the name spread like wildfire.

2
The Challenge Cup, presented by *The Field* magazine, was valued at 25 guineas and the first winner, Spencer Gore, held it for one year. Apart from Challenge trophies, the 1976 winner Björn Borg collected £12,500.

THE CHAMPION LAWN TENNIS MATCH: MR. HARTLEY WINNING THE CUP FOR THE SECOND TIME.

3
Back in 1877, spectators used Wimbledon as a vehicle for showing off their best clothes. Despite infiltration by casual present-day youngsters, the championships retain a fashion-conscious ambience.

4
It rained occasionally even in the rosy days of 1879. And men already knew the value of volleying.

5
1880: J.T. Hartley winning the men's singles for the second time but how did that spelling mistake in Lawford's name escape the referee?

Harrow cricket match at Lords was scheduled for 12 July and its rival attractions as a crowd-puller had to be acknowledged.

Heathcote, Jones, and Marshall were appointed to draw up the rules and they began a study of the many differing sets then in existence. Deciding that none of them was suitable, they drew up a completely new set. So skilled were their decisions that those rules have, in essence, remained in operation ever since.

Three in particular seemed revolutionary. They ignored Wingfield's specification of a court shaped like an hourglass and stipulated a rectangular court 26 yards long and 9 yards wide. They adopted in its entirety the scoring system of the ancient

game of Real Tennis (in Australia – Royal Tennis; in the United States – Court Tennis), allowing the server one fault. And the height of the net was fixed at 5 feet at the posts and 3 feet 3 inches in the middle.

This latter ruling was to prove decisive in Gore's triumph. He realized that the height of the net at the posts severely handicapped straight shots and that the majority of returns would be across the court. Armed with that theory, he ran forward to the net at every possible opportunity, there to exploit his flexibility of wrist with angled volleys that evaded his opponents first on one side, then on the other. So eager and severe were his net sorties, and those of the men who

emulated him, that by the 1880 championship a rule had been introduced which forbad the striking of the ball before it crossed the net: so much for the widespread belief that net play is a modern invention.

In fact the answer to net-rushing came in 1878 when P.F. Hadow thoughtfully realized the alternative of altitude. Thus the final-day crowd of 700 saw him repulse Gore's net attacks with shrewd returns which sent the ball 18 feet up above the ground before it landed somewhere in the region of Gore's baseline. The lob was born, and the never-ending swing, first in favour of attack, then of defence, begun.

In 1879, 1,100 saw J.T. Hartley beat V. Gould, maybe

prophetically for Hartley was a clergyman and Gould the only Wimbledon finalist ever to be convicted of murder. Despite the growing number of spectators, tennis's future was by no means secure. Gore may have been, in modern parlance, a 'net-rusher' but Hadow's invention of the lob had swung the balance in favour of defence and there was much talk of a 'pat-ball' game.

Little-known A.T. Myers introduced the overarm service to Wimbledon in 1879 but his defeat in the second round probably obscured its potential as a dominating weapon. Though not from twins William and Ernest Renshaw, two of the most inventive players in history. Adventurous and imaginative, they enjoyed power and aggression. The earliest service aces – services which the receiver cannot even touch – came from their rackets. They discovered the answer to the lob, making the volleying base nearer to the service line than the net, and they converted men's doubles into the most exciting spectator experience by introducing the 'both men at the net' system. Strangely, they were not

themselves fully convinced of its superiority. William even went so far as to write a letter to *The Field*, dated 26 May 1883, advocating the old 'one man at the net, one back on the baseline' orthodox pattern then in general use. But he and his brother negated this advice by winning the doubles in 1884 and on four subsequent occasions.

Could this criticism of their own methods have been the first case of gamesmanship or mental warfare on potential rivals? Almost certainly not, for those were the days of Olympic idealism in tennis, as H.S. Barlow demonstrated so dramatically when playing William in the 1889 All-Comers' Final. Within one point of defeat and scrambling desperately to counter Barlow's attack, William slipped and lost his racket. Instead of quietly placing the ball into the open court, Barlow lofted it high, allowing William time to recover his feet and racket and continue the rally. William saved this and five more match points before winning the match and then the Challenge Round against the holder, his brother Ernest.

6
1880 and increasing crowds necessitated a grandstand. Note the name above it. F.H. Ayres dominated tennis until 1903, when the Slazenger ball was first adopted for the championships, a tenure which the company has retained ever since.

7
William Renshaw on the way to a 1-6, 6-3, 6-2, 5-6, 6-3 semi-final win over H.F. Lawford (left) in the 1881 championships. Neither the advantage set nor the 12-point tie-breaker had been dreamed of in those days. The former came in the following year.

8
An artist's impression of the 1883 championships. The public have been given a bigger stand than three years earlier and the umpire was so conscientious that to obtain a better view he stood on his stool instead of sitting.

6

THE LAWN TENNIS CHAMPIONSHIP MEETING AT WIMBLEDON—THE FIFTH ROUND OF THE ALL COMERS' MATCH 1881

CHAMPIONSHIP-MEETING, 1883   AT THE ALL ENGLAND LAWN-TENNIS CLUB GROUND, WIMBLEDON

E. de S. H. Browne   Rev. J. T. Hartley *(Champion 1879, 1880)*   C. W. Grinstead   Miss Maud Watson *(Lady Champion)*   H. F. Lawford *(Irish Champion, Winner of Wimbledon Gold Prize, 1884)*   W. Renshaw *(Champion 1881, 1882, 1883, 1884)*

E. Renshaw *(Winner of Wimbledon Gold Prize, 1882, 1883)*   Miss Watson

SOME ENGLISH LAWN-TENNIS PLAYERS

LAWN-TENNIS CHAMPIONSHIP MATCHES AT WIMBLEDON 1887

9
Eight stars of the early days

10
Impressions of the 1887 championships. Blanche Bingley and Lottie Dod are not foot faulting. In those days the server had to keep one foot on the baseline. Miss Dod never adopted the overarm service though she had a strong smash.

From 1877 through to 1922 each winner of the championship was excused playing through the next year. Instead he (or she after 1885) sat by until the winner of the All-Comers' Singles came through to challenge for the championship. This was a fairly common practice at the time but Wimbledon was on its march towards sporting immortality. No aspect escaped close scrutiny and tradition took second place to effectiveness.

That forward march provided early evidence that the old ground in Worple Road could not for ever contain the expanding championships. The year 1883 saw the arrival of the first entries from the USA, the brothers C.M. and J.S. Clark. One year later Miss Maud Watson won the inaugural ladies' championship, and the men's doubles championship, founded at Oxford University in

1879, transferred to Wimbledon. A count of strokes played in the All-Comers' Final between H.F. Lawford and C.W. Grinstead revealed 102 volleys and 479 groundstrokes. The crowds still grew, 3,500 watching the 1885 Challenge Round in which William Renshaw beat H.F. Lawford. Maud Watson retained the ladies' title that year but she lost it to Blanche Bingley in 1886, the year in which Charlotte 'Lottie' Dod, then only fourteen years old, proved herself the equal of the four top ladies in the country.

One year later, aged fifteen years and ten months, Lottie Dod won the Wimbledon singles, a feat she repeated on another four occasions before retiring from competitive tennis at the age of twenty-one because of boredom with the ease of her wins and the absence of strong opposition. Turning her talents to other activities, she played hockey for England in 1889 and 1890 and won the British Ladies' Golf Championship in 1904 when still only thirty-two years old. She could remain the youngest ever women's Wimbledon winner since there is now an internationally agreed rule setting a lower age limit of sixteen in the world's major international championships.

Still untouched by the cult of the individual, Wimbledon's popularity grew steadily, and ticket scalpers could be found on many final days. The pre-1900 years featured many family successes, the Renshaws, Baddeleys, and Dohertys coming quickly to mind.

The reign of the Renshaws extended from 1881 to 1889, only the year 1887 producing another champion, H.F. Lawford. Willie won the singles seven times in all and his brother Ernest once, in 1888. To William goes the honour of winning the shortest men's final in the history of the championships: in 1881, when he took only 37 minutes to beat the holder, the Reverend Hartley, in the Challenge Round. The score was 6-0, 6-2, 6-1 and Renshaw was then aged only twenty.

11
Joshua Pim, winner of the men's singles in 1893 and 1894. A doctor, he was born in Ireland and was, technically, the first 'foreign' champion.

12
A key match during the 1884 championships. Both men are in back court but a check carried out revealed that in singles the ratio of volleys to groundstrokes was 1 to 4·75. This differs little from today.

THE ALL-ENGLAND LAWN TENNIS CHAMPIONSHIPS.

MRS. HILLYARD, WINNER LADIES' SINGLES FOR 111TH TIME.   MISS C. COOPER, CHALLENGER (THREE TIMES WINNER).   MRS. HILLYARD.

MR. H. S. SMITH, CHALLENGER GENTLEMEN'S SINGLES.

MR. R. F. DOHERTY, WINNER GENTLEMEN'S SINGLES FOR THE FOURTH SUCCESSIVE TIME.

14

13
Stars of the championships in 1900. Mrs Hillyard won the singles six times in all, hat notwithstanding, Chattie Cooper five times, and Reggie Doherty four times. S.H. Smith reached the Challenge Round but never won it.

14
Blanche Bingley, later Mrs George Hillyard, captured the women's singles title six times between the years 1886 and 1900.

15
George Hillyard (left), a doubles finalist and championship secretary, with H.L. Doherty, five times singles champion and holder of the all-time best Davis Cup record.

16
Improvised seating sufficed in 1895, but the spectators still sported their finest clothes. Notice how up to date the net and post height appear.

Wilfred Baddeley won the singles three times and with his brother Herbert, the doubles twice. To Wilfred goes the record of the youngest ever men's singles winner, his title-winning bid in 1891 coming when he was only nineteen years old. Lottie Dod, the woman champion of the year, was also only nineteen, so that destroys any myth that youth was never so dominant as in the late 1970s.

The Dohertys ruled the roost from 1897 to 1906, Reginald, the older brother, winning the title in '97, '98, '99, and 1900, and his brother Laurie taking the singles in 1902, 1903, 1904, 1905, and 1906. Poor health cost Reginald the title in 1901 when he lost his crown to Arthur Wentworth Gore who, earlier, survived a matched point against George Hillyard, the club secretary. But together the Dohertys won the doubles by beating Dwight Davis, donor of the famous cup, and Holcombe Ward, both of the USA. It was in 1901 that Wimbledon became truly international. (Gore repeated his triumph on two other occasions, his third win coming in 1909

when forty-one years and six months of age, so he holds the record of the oldest Wimbledon singles champion.)

Ladies had made their debut in 1884, Maud Watson beating her sister Lillian to become the first singles champion. Daughter of a Cambridge clergyman, Maud benefited from extensive practice against male opponents, as did Lottie Dod later. Marriages, too, maintained the somewhat closed community. Blanche Bingley, six times champion, won once in her maiden name and five times more as wife of George Hillyard.

17

1. THE AMERICAN WINNER OF THE LADIES' CHAMPION-
SHIP: MISS MAY SUTTON PLAYING BACK.

2. AN AUSTRALIAN'S VICTORY IN THE GENTLEMEN'S SINGLES:
NORMAN BROOKES (IN FOREGROUND) DEFEATS GORE.

3. THE LADY CHAMPION FOR 1907: MISS MAY SUTTON'S
BACKHANDED SERVICE.

4. AUSTRALIA BEATS AMERICA IN THE GENTLEMEN'S DOUBLES: BROOKES AND WILDING
DEFEAT BEHR AND WRIGHT (IN FOREGROUND).

5. THE FINAL FOR THE LADIES' SINGLE CHAMPIONSHIP: MISS SUTTON (NEAREST) BEATS
MRS. LAMBERT CHAMBERS, THE HOLDER.

18

19

18

It was in 1901 that Wimbledon became truly international, but players from the British Isles maintained their domination until 1905 when Norman Brookes of Australia and May Sutton of the USA became the all-comers' and outright champions respectively. Both were highly competitive yet Wimbledon retained its Olympic spirit and even the champions were spared the idolatry enjoyed by quite mediocre contenders of the present day.

Charlotte Cooper, later Mrs Alfred Sterry, emphasized the point after winning the women's singles in 1893. Cycling happily home after her triumph, she sped down Ewell Road, Surbiton, turned into the family home and cheerfully put the bike to bed . . . in the chicken run. On the way indoors she heard Uncle Fred, busily snipping the wisteria, call out, 'Where have you been?' Told she had been playing tennis at Wimbledon, he asked, still snipping, 'How did you get on?' 'I won' she said to an unimpressed uncle, who continued the dialogue by asking if she would make him a cup of tea. The Sterrys and the Coopers were, incidentally, part of a tennis dynasty which survives in Wimbledon's hundredth year through Charlotte's son, Rex Sterry, the championships' vice chairman, and nephew Tony Cooper, curator of the museum

17
Moments from the 1907 championships. The vigorous lady in the top row is May Sutton who, in 1905, became the first American champion. Norman Brookes, the first Australian winner, is the left hander, his opponent Arthur Gore.

18
Arthur Wentworth Gore, singles champion in 1901, 1908 and 1909. His last win came at the age of forty-one, so he is the oldest singles champion in history.

19
Norman Brookes, with his flat-topped racket and vicious spinning and serving, took the title home to Melbourne, Australia, in 1907.

20
Miss Maud Coles in play at the 1910 championships. Her grand-niece, Glynis Coles, is a top British contender in the centenary meeting.

21
Arthur Gore, near end, strenuously challenging the holder Tony Wilding in the 1912 final, won by Wilding in four 10-game sets.

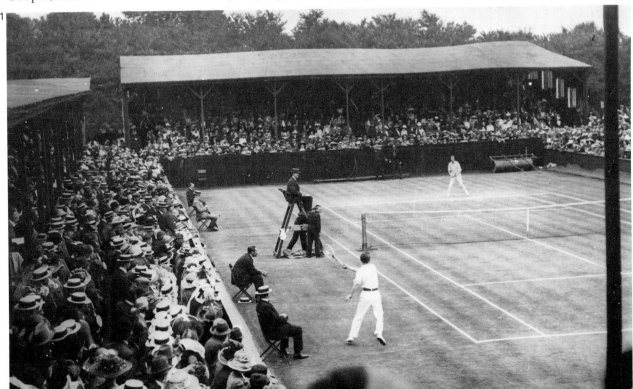

QUEENS OF THE TOURNAMENT: FAMOUS LAWN-TENNIS PLAYERS.

PHOTOGRAPHS BY SPORT AND GENERAL.

1. MRS. O'NEILL.	4. MRS. SATTERTHWAITE.	7. MRS. TUCKEY.	10. MISS H. AITCHISON.	13. MISS HOLMAN.
2. MRS. PARTON.	5. MISS TULLOCH.	8. MRS. STERRY.	11. MRS. LAMBERT CHAMBERS.	14. MRS. MACNAIR.
3. MRS. HANNAM.	6. MRS. HILLYARD.	9. MRS. EDGINGTON.	12. MRS. LARCOMBE.	15. MISS D. P. BOOTHBY.

22

Famous contenders for the 1913 ladies' singles championship

opened in May 1977 as part of the centenary celebrations.

Norman Brookes, later Sir Norman, was back in 1907, winning the Challenge Round by default when Laurie Doherty failed to enter. That was the year when all the titles went abroad for the first time. A particular mark of royal interest was bestowed on Wimbledon in that year when the Prince of Wales, later George V, paid his first visit to the championships. Subsequently he not only accepted the presidency of the All England Club, but also presented the handsome cup which is still held annually by the winner of the men's singles. The prince and his wife were piloted to their seats in the committee box by the new club secretary, Commander George Hillyard RN. Thus began a dual patronage which was to last almost thirty years in the case of the prince and two full generations in the case of the then princess, later to become Queen Mary.

The year 1910 heralded a completely new approach to tennis, an approach which was not fully emulated until the era of Harry Hopman as Australia's non-playing Davis Cup captain after World War II. Anthony Wilding, a New Zealander nicknamed Little Hercules at the age of two, won the men's singles title for the first time, bringing a serious dedication to the game that was entirely new. An undergraduate at Cambridge, Wilding had determined to improve his backhand during the winter of 1909-10 so he badgered the municipal authorities at Cambridge to let him improvise a court in the Corn Exchange. There he and his friends swept away the remnants of the vegetable market on many afternoons before settling down to the practice which remodelled Wilding's backhand, so enabling him to survive the pounding it received during his Wimbledon campaign in the June and July of 1910. Wilding's clean-living, persistent training and assiduous practice to eliminate weaknesses won him a tremendous reputation and hosts of good friends wherever he travelled. His superb fitness helped him wait out storms of skilled attacks before hitting back with devastating offensives of his own.

23
Tony Wilding, the forerunner of the Björn Borg era, signing autographs for female fans during the 1914 championships

24
With war clouds gathering, vast crowds found momentary forgetfulness at Wimbledon during the 1914 championships.

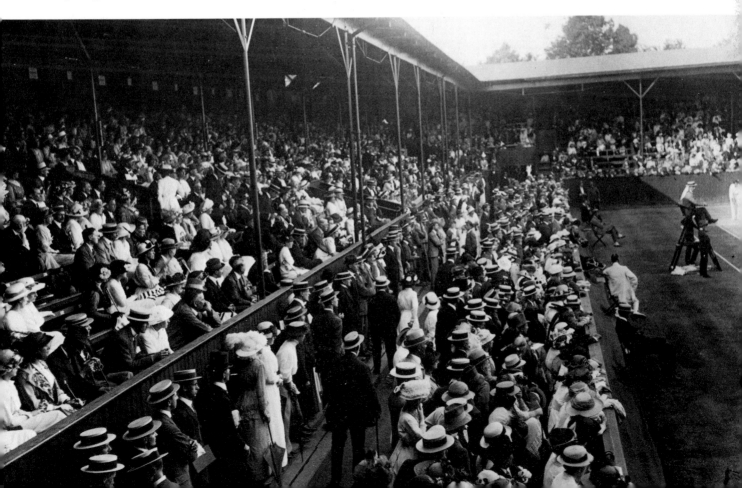

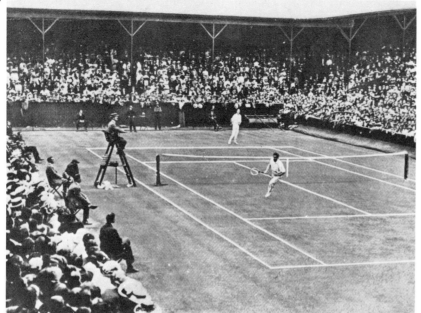

25
Maurice McLoughlin, near end, introduced the cannonball service into tennis and arrived for the 1913 championships with a formidable reputation. Tony Wilding, far end, withstood the challenge.

26
Elizabeth Ryan never won the singles but she collected nineteen Wimbledon titles in doubles, a record equalled by Billie Jean King.

Perhaps Wilding's greatest victory was in the Challenge Round of 1913 when he met and overcame the legendary American Maurice McLoughlin, the originator of the cannonball service which is so commonplace today. The hope of a superb contest caught the public imagination and ticket scalpers asked and received £10 each for Centre Court tickets (relatively topping the prices asked by touts today). Well as McLoughlin served in that final, it was Wilding's supremely accurate returns of service, low and acutely angled to the incoming volleyer's backhand, which controlled the play. Holding set point at 5-4, McLoughlin delivered a thunderbolt to the backhand and Wilding clouted it straight down the line for an outright winning passing shot. McLoughlin, a brilliant player and tenacious fighter, held on for an 8-6, 6-3, 10-8 score yet without ever seriously threatening to overcome the holder.

The gathering clouds of World War I failed to stop the committee from extending the stand to accommodate an extra 1,200 spectators in 1914. Meanwhile, Wilding, sportingly, and others had been pressing for the abolition of the Challenge Round, a move supported by the Lawn Tennis Association. A poll

27
Dorothea Lambert Chambers winning the ladies' singles for the seventh time: her victim in the 1914 final, Mrs D.R. Larcombe.

of 142 principal players voted: abolish 68, retain 46, no answer 26. Nevertheless, it was not until 1922 when 91 out of 118 players voted for the holder taking part in the first round that the Challenge Round principle was abandoned.

It was in 1914 that Wilding was finally overcome – by the magnificently varied and effective serving of Norman Brookes. The 1914 All-Comers' Final saw Brookes oust German-born Otto Froitzheim 6-2, 6-1, 5-7, 4-6, 8-6, a tussle which seemed almost an omen of the war to come. Yet such were the sporting traditions of tennis that when Froitzheim was taken prisoner of war, he wrote to secretary George Hillyard, asking him to use his influence to have him freed as it was unsporting to keep him from fighting for his country. The request was not taken up.

A seventh success and a then record came to Mrs Lambert Chambers of Great Britain when she won the ladies' singles from fellow countrywoman Mrs Larcombe in the same year.

Between the Wars

So the championship gates closed for five long years, but thanks largely to the personal efforts of H. Wilson-Fox, president from 1915–21, the club was kept going and it proved possible to resume the championships in 1919. That year entries were so numerous, 128 in all, that selection had to be considered. Additionally, applications for tickets had grown so enormously that the now-famous ballot was introduced. These were both healthy signs that Wimbledon, despite the interruption of the war, would prove more popular than ever. And so it was. As a reunion of players and patrons from all over the world, the championships were a remarkable success and the final seal of greatness was applied with two visits to the royal box by George V and Queen Mary. Financially too the championships surpassed all previous records, with gate receipts rising by £2,390 from the £7,000 of 1914.

Truthfully, however, the play in these championships was not up to the standards later attained. But this was not unexpected: the majority of the competitors had after all been engaged in war service. However, the ladies' Challenge Round may well have atoned since it produced probably the greatest ladies' singles final in the entire 100 years of the championships.

Mrs Lambert Chambers, already seven times champion, was there to defend her crown. But it was Mademoiselle Suzanne Lenglen, a stocky, swarthy, full-bosomed, twenty-year-old French-woman of immense personality, who caught the popular fancy. Well on 8,000 people, including

28

28
Suzanne Lenglen heralded the era of the cult of the personality when she came and conquered in 1919. Compare her dress with that of Mrs Lambert Chambers opposite.

the King, Queen, and Princess Mary turned up for her meeting with Dorothea Lambert Chambers in the Challenge Round. Nineteen years had slipped by since Mrs Lambert Chambers had first won the title

and time should have taken its toll. Maybe it did a little, but Mrs Chambers remained a great player and an indomitable fighter.

After a see-saw battle with first one player and then the other gaining the ascendancy, Mrs Chambers reached 6-5 and 40-15 in the final set. Never flinching, Suzanne hit deep to the forehand and raced for the net. Alert to the move, Mrs Chambers

29

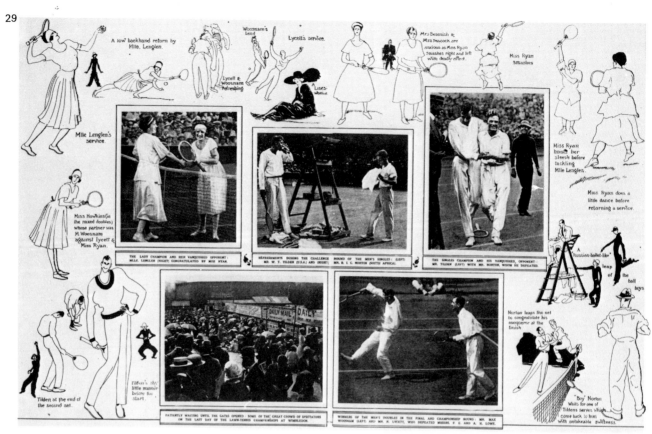

A low backhand return by Mlle. Lenglen.

Woosnam's bend.

Lycett's service.

Lycett & Woosnam refreshing.

"Lines" woman.

Mrs Beamish & Mrs Peacock are anxious as Miss Ryan Smashes right and left with deadly effect.

Miss Ryan Smashes.

Mile Lenglen's service.

Miss Howkins (in the mixed doubles) whose partner was M. Woosnam against Lycett & Miss Ryan.

Miss Ryan boosts her sleeve before tackling Mlle Lenglen.

Miss Ryan does a little dance before returning a service.

Tilden's shy little manner before the start.

Tilden at the end of the second set.

A "Russian-ballet-like" leap of the ball boys.

Norton leaps the net to congratulate his conqueror at the finish.

"Boy" Norton waits for one of Tilden's serves which come back to him with unfakeable swiftness.

THE LADY CHAMPION AND HER VANQUISHED OPPONENT: MLLE. LENGLEN (RIGHT) CONGRATULATED BY MISS RYAN.

REFRESHMENTS DURING THE CHALLENGE ROUND OF THE MEN'S SINGLES: (LEFT) MR. W. T. TILDEN (U.S.A.) AND (RIGHT) MR. B. I. C. NORTON (SOUTH AFRICA).

THE SINGLES CHAMPION AND HIS VANQUISHED OPPONENT: MR. TILDEN (LEFT) WITH MR. NORTON, WHOM HE DEFEATED.

PATIENTLY WAITING UNTIL THE GATES OPENED: SOME OF THE GREAT CROWD OF SPECTATORS ON THE LAST DAY OF THE LAWN-TENNIS CHAMPIONSHIPS AT WIMBLEDON.

WINNERS OF THE MEN'S DOUBLES IN THE FINAL AND CHAMPIONSHIP ROUND: MR. MAX WOOSNAM (LEFT) AND MR. R. LYCETT, WHO DEFEATED MESSRS. F. G. AND A. H. LOWE.

30

24

sent over a lob that appeared to be clearing Suzanne. Leaping backwards, Suzanne threw up her racket and caught the ball near to the frame. Had she anticipated this lucky reply, Mrs Chambers would surely have scored with a placement in Suzanne's open court, but she was left flat-footed in surprise. Thus reprieved, Suzanne hit boldly with her backhand to save the second match point. Though the tension and superb tennis were maintained to the end, Suzanne never again looked in danger of defeat and she took the title 10-8, 4-6, 9-7.

The following year heralded the arrival of Mr Tennis, William

Tatem Tilden of the USA, reckoned by the majority of experts to have been the greatest player in the history of the game. The records show that other men took part; the entry exceeded 128 and so necessitated selection by a special committee. But they were virtually non-existent so far as press and public were concerned for only Tilden and Suzanne Lenglen seemed worthy of real interest.

Seeding – the placing of the best players in different parts of the draw so that they cannot meet until the later rounds – had not yet been introduced and the draw worked out terribly, with Tilden and his primary

challengers all in the same half. Tilden survived the many challenges and went on to beat Zenzo Schimidzu of Japan in the final and Gerald Patterson of Australia, the holder, in the Challenge Round. This win marked a new era for it ended the reign of the serve-volley specialists and demonstrated that the great players of the future would have to be as sound from the baseline as they were at the net. As has been the case so often at Wimbledon and in the other major championships, the strength of return of service earned as many key games as Tilden's railroad serving and incisive volleying.

29
The last Wimbledon at Worple Road, 1921, produced Suzanne Lenglen and Bill Tilden as the two singles champions.

30
'Big Bill' Tilden winning Wimbledon at his first try in 1921, but he was within one point of losing to 'Babe' Norton in the Challenge Round.

31
Not only the young besieged Suzanne Lenglen for her autograph. Suzanne introduced the bandeau which is back in fashion though in a narrower, decorated form.

31

32 another show court, No. 1, with
a capacity of 5,000. There were
two further display courts,
flanked by stands from the old
Wimbledon. All those courts
have been extended in their
spectator capacities and other
show courts have since been
established but, essentially, the
Wimbledon of 1977 is very much
like the Wimbledon of 1922 . . .
and in more ways than this. Rain
spoilt much of the play and the
final of the men's singles did not
take place until the third
Monday of the championships.
Gerald Patterson beat Randolph
Lycett, another Australian
although resident in England, in
the men's singles final and
Suzanne Lenglen avenged the
only defeat she ever suffered in
singles after World War I, by
thrashing Mrs Molla Mallory
6-2, 6-0. They went on court for
this final at 1 minute past 7 late
one afternoon and came off at
26 minutes past 7.

This domination of the
women's singles by a French lady
undoubtedly inspired a now
legendary group of four men in
France: Jean Borotra, Jean-René
Lacoste, Henri Cochet, and
Jacques Brugnon. Borotra,
Lacoste, and Cochet each won
the singles on two occasions
between 1924 and 1929. The year
1927 produced the worst weather
in Wimbledon history, the
championships taking fourteen
days to play instead of the usual

32
The late King George V and Queen
Mary, attending the first match at
the new Wimbledon. They saw
Leslie Godfree serve a fault, rush to
the net, and put the ball in his
trouser pocket. Moths ate this
souvenir during World War Ii.

33
The French era began in 1924 when
Jean Borotra, left, beat René
Lacoste in the final, a defeat
avenged one year later.

34
Jacques Brugnon (left) and Henri
Cochet leaving the Centre Court as
the 1926 doubles champions.

35
Christian Boussus, right, pictured
with Bill Tilden. A stylish left-
hander, Boussus never quite
achieved the greatness of the
'Musketeers'.

Suzanne, a more complete and
confident player than when she
overthrew Mrs Lambert
Chambers in 1919, retained her
title with ease, beating Mrs
Lambert Chambers in the
Challenge Round 6-3, 6-0.

The writing on the wall could
no longer be obscured. The old
Wimbledon at Worple Road was
no longer large enough and a
new centre had to be found. It
was – at Church Road,
Wimbledon, and building of the
new complex began. It opened
on 26 June 1922, George V
officiating. This imposing
monument to tennis was the
creation of Captain Stanley
Peach and it featured the
magnificent Centre Court with a
capacity of over 14,000 and

twelve and occasional thirteen of recent years. The same year saw the introduction of a complete seeding system in all the events.

Attendances broke all standing records in 1928, and in 1930 Bill Tilden, champion in 1920 and 1921, set the seal on his amazing career by winning the singles at the age of thirty-eight. The other main feature of this meeting was the USA's complete domination, her players capturing all five events.

It was the distinction of 1931 to be the year without a men's singles final, Sidney Wood gaining his title because his fellow American Frank Shields had slipped in the semi-final and damaged his knee. A German girl, Fräulein Cilly Aussem, won the women's singles. American Ellsworth Vines was the man of 1932; his play in the last three rounds is believed by many who saw it to have been the finest tennis ever produced anywhere by any man in the history of the game. Certainly never before or after did he achieve such greatness.

The weather and his opponents helped enormously, but two examples of his power illustrate how fearsome he was. The first came early in the championships when one of his overhead smashes resulted in a ball hitting a ball-boy in the chest and knocking him head-over-heels. The other came at match point in the men's singles final against Great Britain's Bunny Austin. Vines threw up the ball, served, and the next thing Austin knew was the thump of the ball as it hit the back canvas. At his club in South London the next morning, he vowed: 'I saw him swing his racket and I heard the ball hit the back canvas. The umpire called game, set and match, so I knew it was all over but I never saw the ball.'

36
A contemporary artist's impression of the abundantly attended 1932 championships

37
Britain's Bunny Austin reached the final but never even saw the tremendous service ace with which Ellsworth Vines took the last point. Austin ended the year second in the world rankings.

36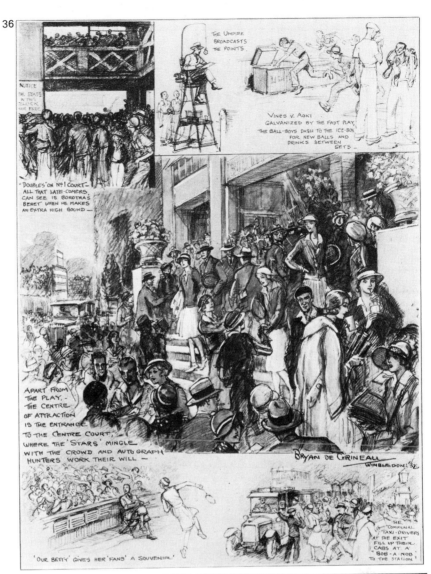

37

Vines appeared invincible but Australian Jack Crawford, whom Vines had annihilated in the 1932 semi-final, was a keen student of the game. He made an intense study of his opponent and practised tactics which he believed could overthrow this formidable but thoroughly sporting, lanky American. Seeded in opposite halves of the draw in 1933, they went through to the final and when Vines took the first set 6-4, the majority of spectators already believed him to be champion. They were wrong. Crawford's clever aggression against Vines's formidable forehand and his immaculate returns of service gradually swung the day. Winning the 20-game second set, he took the third 6-2, before dropping the fourth by the same score. The fifth set will surely live forever in the minds of those who saw it. It was the rapier versus the bludgeon, and at four games all, no-one could tell who would triumph. Crawford held his service for 5-4 and then, raising his game to supreme heights, secured the final service break to capture the title everyone thought beyond his capabilities.

Britain had a great year in 1934 with Fred Perry winning the men's singles for the first of his run of three. Perry beat Jack Crawford in this final, and then in 1935 and 1936 scored two victories over Gottfried von Cramm, in 1936 by 6-1, 6-1, 6-0 in a final which lasted only 42 minutes. Von Cramm damaged a muscle in the second game.

Simultaneously in 1934, Dorothy Round won the women's singles, a feat she was to repeat in 1937. With Britain dominant in the Davis Cup, the challenge rounds of which were played at Wimbledon, these were halcyon days for British tennis.

They ended when Perry turned professional to play a series of matches against Vines. This left a giant, red-headed Californian, Don Budge, as the supreme figure in men's international tennis. In 1937 Budge set up a new record by becoming the first to win all three Wimbledon titles open to a man in one year.

38

39

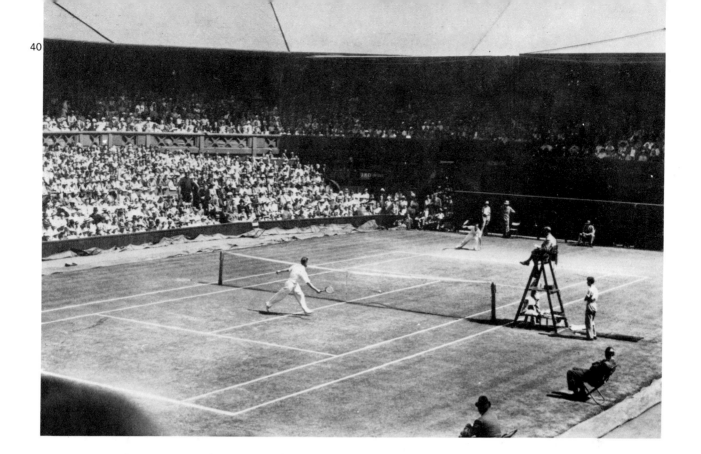

40

41

42

38
Jack Crawford gaining a superbly conceived, upset victory over Ellsworth Vines in the 1933 final, judged by many to be the finest match ever seen

39
Vines fought bitterly before yielding in a 10-game fifth set.

40
Fred Perry, far end, on his way to victory over Jack Crawford in the 1934 final

41
Dorothy Round, British winner of the singles in 1934 and 1937, with the dazzling Senorita Lily de Alvarez in 1931

42
Fred Perry, the only British man champion since 1909. He won in 1934, 1935 and 1936.

He went even better in 1938 when he took the singles without loss of a solitary set as well as retaining the other two championships. Not since 1925, when Suzanne Lenglen won the women's singles for the loss of only five games in ten sets, had anyone been so completely superior to all the opposition.

Professional tennis, with its lucrative guarantees, was growing ever more attractive to the world's top stars and Budge followed Perry's example by turning professional at the end of 1938. He was succeeded in 1939 by another American, Bobby Riggs, who also won all three titles, and reputedly earned a small fortune by backing himself to do so at long odds.

43
Baron Gottfried von Cramm and Donald Budge come on court for the 1937 final, won by Budge. It was the beginning of a wonderful friendship.

44
Alice Marble (left) and Britain's Kay Stammers before the 1939 final, won by Miss Marble 6-2, 6-0, a deceptive score for they both produced superb tennis

45
Bobbie Riggs, winner of all three events in 1939. A subtle player, his skill forced later Americans to modify their ideas significantly.

Towards the First Century

The war clouds were again gathering and the storm broke in September, so closing the championships until 1946 but never the club, even though the Centre Court suffered severe damage from enemy bombing. Play resumed in 1945, when a couple of international matches celebrating victory, one the British Empire versus the USA, were staged on Court No. 1.

The championships returned to life to the glee of players and spectators alike. Except for the still bomb-damaged Centre Court stand, the All England Club looked no different and the courts appeared better than ever.

Inevitably, the general standard of play was somewhat lower than usual, but there was no lacking in keenness. In the interim years both Riggs and fellow American Alice Marble, the 1939 champions, had turned professional. Jack Kramer, who had represented the United States in the 1939 Davis Cup Challenge Round, was the favourite to win.

But a blistered hand proved a severe handicap and this helped Frenchman Yvon Petra to take the singles. Pauline Betz beat fellow American Louise Brough in the women's final and began an American domination of this event that lasted right through until 1959, when Maria Bueno took the title home to Brazil. Kramer returned to win the men's singles in 1947, followed it by taking the American Championship, and then turned professional.

46
War or no war, play continued at Wimbledon, even though fire bombs damaged the Centre Court stands.

47
Jack Kramer, champion in 1947 and number four among the all-time greats. As executive director of the Association of Tennis Professionals, he led the 1973 boycott of over seventy major stars yet few love Wimbledon more than him.

48

50
Maureen Connolly, second youngest ever Wimbledon champion, known affectionately as 'Little Mo'

50

48
Finalists in the 1951 men's doubles: left to right K. McGregor and F. Sedgman (both Australia), J. Drobny (Egypt) and E. Sturgess (South Africa)

49
Royalty at Wimbledon. HRH Prince Philip presents the cup to the 1957 champion, Lew Hoad. Ashley Cooper, the loser, went one better in 1958.

49

Thirty different nations competed in 1948, and 1949 was undoubtedly the most exciting of the four post-war Wimbledons. The USA almost made a clean sweep of everything, but they were hard pressed in so doing. Indeed only Ted Schroeder's propensity for saving match points obscured the true position. He saved three of them against the rapidly rising Australian Frank Sedgman, in the singles quarter-finals, and then in partnership with American Gardnar Mulloy saved further match points against the Australians Geoff Brown and Bill Sidwell, who looked certain of taking the men's doubles.

Americans continued to dominate in 1950, but in 1951 the forthcoming ascendancy of Australia was foreshadowed when Ken McGregor reached the singles final where he was beaten by American Dick Savitt. But he won the men's doubles with Frank Sedgman, while Sedgman and Doris Hart of America beat the Australians Mervyn Rose and Nancy Bolton in the mixed doubles final.

Three young players, Maureen Connolly, Lewis Hoad, and Ken Rosewall, all destined to make tennis history, entered the scene for the first time in the 1952 championships. Despite their tender years, all came to Wimbledon with great reputations which they fully sustained with brilliant play.

Chief honours went to Miss Connolly of the USA, who won the championship at her first attempt. She repeated this feat in 1953 and again in 1954 before a serious riding accident ended her international career.

51
Ken Rosewall, four times runner-up but never the champion. His span covers twenty-five years of Wimbledon . . . Not out!

52
Louise Brough, winner of eight events out of nine in the years 1948 to 1950, and runner-up in the ninth: a stupendous record.

53
Budge Patty: he abandoned a playboy attitude for the year 1950 and was rewarded with the singles championship.

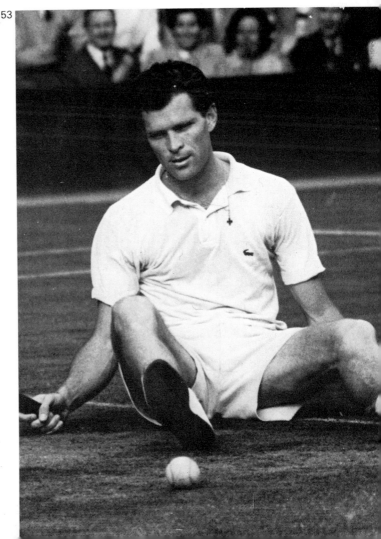

Rosewall, an Australian, was fated never to win the singles, although he reached the final four times in a span at Wimbledon which lasted from 1952 through to 1975 and it seems likely he will continue competing for a few years yet.

Fellow Australian Hoad won in 1956 and produced astonishing play to retain the title in 1957 before turning professional on the final Saturday night of the championships. In the same year American Althea Gibson made history by becoming the first Black player to win a championship. And for Britain, Christine Truman, then only sixteen, battled her way to the semi-finals.

Sweden took her first ever title in 1958 when Sven Davidson and Ulf Schmidt won the men's doubles. Such was the importance of the Wimbledon championships that the captain of the Swedish boat scheduled to return Davidson and Schmidt to their home country on the Saturday morning, delayed the boat's departure until a later tide so that the two stars could play the final.

The years 1960 through to 1967 were saturated by world-wide campaigns to make tennis a game open to both amateurs and professionals. From the beginning the Wimbledon championships were open only to amateurs, who quite early in tennis history began receiving under-the-table payments elsewhere. However, it is fitting that Wimbledon's ever active and enterprising committees were in the van of those pressing for honesty in tennis.

In 1966 Santana gave Spain her first win in the men's singles, and in 1967 Herman David, chairman of the club and the championships' committee, first obtained the unanimous approval of club members to launch a bombshell on the world: whether the International Lawn Tennis Federation approved or not, the Wimbledon championships of 1968 would be open to all categories of tennis players. He had a reasonable certainty that the championships would succeed, for in 1967, following an appeal from the 1947 champion Jack Kramer, he had agreed to the staging of a 'professionals only' championship in August on the Centre Court. This attracted large crowds and produced an encouraging profit.

54
Althea Gibson, the first Black player to win a Wimbledon title. She beat Darlene Hard in the final.

55
Gardnar Mulloy (left) and Budge Patty surprised and delighted sentimental fans by winning the doubles in 1957.

56
Triumph for Sweden. Ulf Schmidt (left) and Sven Davidson winning the 1958 doubles final

56

54

55

57

58

59

60

57
Angela Mortimer ends Britain's twenty-four years in the Wimbledon wilderness by becoming the 1961 singles champion.

58
Runner-up in 1959 and 1960, Rod Laver wins the singles at last and also the congratulations of the late Princess Marina.

59
Down but far from out. Manuel Santana takes a tumble during the 1967 championships but he rose again to become the first Spaniard ever to win one of the world's 'grand slam' singles' crowns. He proved that subtlety can master sheer force.

60
Neale Fraser, right, consoles Rod Laver after the 1960 final, the first ever staged between two left-handed players at Wimbledon. Laver returned to win the title four times in all, twice as an amateur, twice after the game became open to amateurs and professionals alike.

61

62

61
Christine Truman, the idol of the
Wimbledon crowds but never the
champion

62
Maria Bueno, Brazil, probably the
most graceful player ever to adorn
the Centre Court. She won in 1959,
1960 and 1964.

63
A great Australian doubles pair,
Fred Stolle (left) and Bob Hewitt,
champions in 1962 and 1964

64
Karen Susman, USA, champion in
1962

65
Frew McMillan, South Africa, and
Tomus Leijus (right), USSR, show
friendship. The Russian refusal to
play South Africans ended when the
committee told their officials. 'play
or else you will never again be
accepted here'.

63

64

65

67

67
Charles Pasarell, the only man ever to beat the top seed in the first round; the year was 1968, the man Manuel Santana. Pasarell also featured with Pancho Gonzales in the longest match ever played at Wimbledon.

68
Roy Emerson, probably the fittest man ever to play tennis. He won the singles in 1964 and 1965.

69
How to deal with a disobedient ball

69

68

The collapse of the ILTF member countries is now history and the first ever open championship was staged at Bournemouth in 1968: This dress rehearsal foreshadowed perhaps the most exciting Wimbledon to date.

So open tennis came to Wimbledon in 1968 and British fans savoured the opportunity of seeing former great stars like Rod Laver, Ken Rosewall, and Pancho Gonzales back on the courts they had graced anything from five to nineteen years earlier. For the first week the form of these professionals, who had been heralded around the world as the greatest players of all, was somewhat disappointing. But any such feeling gave way to quiet acknowledgement of their superiority in the second week, which ended with the professionals dominating proceedings. Rod Laver of Australia took the men's singles and American Billie Jean King the women's singles. The crowds were high but not so high as in the last year of amateurism, when Australian John Newcombe had taken the title and the attendance for the fortnight had topped the 300,000 mark for the first time.

The year 1969 saw the gathering of storm clouds, principally because of the growing strength of the World Championship Tennis Organization controlled by Texan oil millionaire Lamar Hunt. Hunt had many top players under contract and was able to dictate to them just where they should play. Though all the professionals competed, there was considerable unease between the committee and Lamar Hunt. Sensing difficulties, the players themselves attempted to band together by forming the International Tennis Players Association with John Newcombe as its first president. But the WCT contracts gave them little scope for free action and the association eventually died a natural death. Laver retained his men's singles championship by defeating Newcombe in the final, while in the ladies' singles Britain enjoyed

71

one of her rare triumphs when Ann Jones defeated Billie Jean King in an exciting final.

Over 280,000 enthusiasts watched the eighty-fourth championships in 1970, the third year as an open meeting. British fans, recalling Ann Jones's sterling performances the year before, were filled with fresh hope when Roger Taylor ousted Rod Laver, the winner in 1968

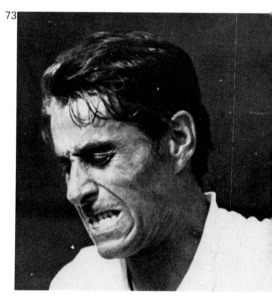

73

72

70
Rod Laver, four times champion, begins his bid for a fifth win. He did not succeed.

71
John Newcombe, three times singles champion and a leader in the 'player power' movement

72
Ken Rosewall en route to the 1970 singles final. Aged thirty-five, he was as nimble as ever but hay fever sapped his stamina in the final.

73
The most thrilling victory Wimbledon has ever known came in 1969 when proud, agonised Pancho Gonzales saved seven match points in a two-day win over Charles Pasarell 22-24, 1-6, 16-14, 6-3, and 11-9.

75

76

74
Already champion in 1966, 1967 and 1968, Billie Jean King wins her 1970 final against Françoise Durr.

75
Policemen guarding the court against anti-apartheid demonstrations while Keith Diepraam plays Jamaican Richard Russell in 1970.

76
Five years have gone since Roy Emerson won the 1965 singles but he still tries harder than anyone.

77
Margaret Court, three times champion and Australia's greatest ever woman player. In centenary year she expects her third child.

77 and 1969, before going through to the semi-final. But it was to be John Newcombe's year. His final victim was Ken Rosewall, who had first reached the singles final as an amateur back in 1954 and then repeated the feat in 1956 when he lost to Lew Hoad. All sentiment was in favour of Rosewall and as he reached two sets all it seemed the miracle might happen but it was not to be. The women's singles final turned out to be one of the greatest in history with Margaret Court of Australia beating Billie Jean King 14–12, 11–9 after a match in which the rallies stayed at a tremendous level of skill and excitement.

Newcombe retained his title in 1971 as expected but the women's event provided a surprise and a delightful champion in Evonne Goolagong. Raised in a small, near outback Australian town, she learned her tennis in her backyard over a rope stretched from a tree, thus proving that Wimbledon champions are not necessarily born with silver spoons in their mouths.

Earlier in the year the French Lawn Tennis Federation had banned the World Championship Tennis professionals from competing in their open in Paris. In 1972 it was to be Wimbledon's turn to impose a ban, those coming under prohibition

including the title-holder John Newcombe plus Rod Laver and Ken Rosewall. Nevertheless Wimbledon managed to preserve its reputation as the world's greatest championship – primarily because of a superb final in which American Stan Smith, the previous year's runner-up, just overcame the magnetic Rumanian Ilie Năstase in a dramatic match staged on the Sunday following the usual closing Saturday.

This was the year the women began to agitate for more recognition and, with it, more pay. Billie Jean King was the mainspring of a number of meetings held during the championships but this seemed to have little effect on her play and she decisively beat Evonne Goolagong of Australia to win the singles for the fourth time in seven finals.

Throughout its history Wimbledon has been noted for politics-free sport but in 1973 all this was changed. It began when Nikki Pilić of Yugoslavia was suspended by his national association for allegedly failing to represent his country in the Davis Cup. The International Lawn Tennis Federation automatically followed suit. Eventually the suspension was severely curtailed, following intensive action by the recently formed Association of Tennis

Professionals, including a law-court hearing in London. But Pilić was not allowed to play at Wimbledon and so over seventy members of ATP staged a boycott of the championships.

Frantic efforts were made to avoid this boycott and the draw for the men's singles was delayed for a couple of days, something unheard of in the clockwork regularity of the Wimbledon organization. Despite the absence of so many great players, or perhaps because of it, the public flocked to Wimbledon and the total attendance of 300,172 was the second highest on record, less than a thousand below the 301,100 who attended the 1967 fortnight. The men's singles went to Jan Kodeš of Czechoslovakia, and Billie Jean King won all three women's events to become the triple champion for the second time in her career.

No one felt the pressure of the boycott more strongly than Roger Taylor. As a member of ATP, he felt honour-bound to go along with their boycott but as a member of the promoting club he felt he had to play. He eventually chose to disregard the boycott and reached the semi-finals. Subsequently he was fined $5,000 by ATP for competing. Mark Cox, the other top-flight British player, made an impassioned speech as a committee member of ATP, asking them not to boycott the championships but when the vote went against him he stood by the association and decided not to enter that year.

The success of Wimbledon in 1973 confirmed the committee's feeling that the championships were still greater than the individuals who played in them. This was in some way

78
Evonne Goolagong, happy-go-lucky, surprise Australian winner in 1971

79
Jan Kodeš, Czechoslovakia, winner in the boycott year, 1973

80
Stan Smith, 1972 champion and a staunch leader of Christians in sport

81
Nikki Pilić in 1971. Two years later his international suspension resulted in over seventy men boycotting Wimbledon.

82
Jimmy Connors and his fiancée, Chris Evert, dominated the 1974 championships. Romance later faded but not their skills.

83
Rosemary Casals never fulfilled herself in singles but in doubles it's been a different story!

82

83

acknowledged unofficially by ATP committee members who disclosed that Wimbledon was chosen for their boycott precisely because it was big enough not to be harmed by their action but also big enough to bring the greatest possible publicity to their claim for justice for one of their members.

Happily everything was restored to normality in time for the 1974 championships. This allowed Wimbledon to set up yet another of its internal records, that of the men's and women's singles being won by two young people who were then engaged to be married, Americans Jimmy Connors and Chris Evert. Another unique feature was that both of them used a double-

handed stroke on their backhand sides. This led to a complete re-think on teaching practices, not only in Britain but all round the world.

With peace in the tennis world re-established, the crowds again flocked to Wimbledon and a new record of 306,161 was set up. Yet overshadowing all this was the superb play of Ken Rosewall in reaching the final for the fourth time, on this occasion twenty years after his first appearance in the tennis year's supreme match. By now he was thirty-nine years old and so his span between the first and this final extended over more than half his lifetime. However, the event was to prove an anticlimax. Rosewall had tired himself

tremendously in three previous matches and was consequently in no fit state to withstand the blistering attack set up by the aggressive young Connors.

If 1974 was the year of Connors, not only at Wimbledon but all round the world, then 1975 was to be that of Arthur Ashe, who defeated Connors in the Wimbledon final with perhaps the cleverest display of tactical tennis ever seen on the famed Centre Court. Connors was an overwhelming favourite but Ashe studied him carefully and knew precisely how to set about overcoming his attacks. Once more crowds flocked to the club, the fortnight's total attendance reaching 338,591, an all-time record.

84
Jimmy Connors, arch exponent of the double-handed backhand stroke

85
Olga Morozova (right) and Virginia Wade. No prizes for guessing who won this 1974 semi-final.

86
Alex Metreveli, in 1973 the first Russian to reach a Wimbledon singles final

Ashe's clever play and the fact
that he was the first Black winner
of the men's singles perhaps
overshadowed an even greater
feat by Billie Jean King, who
won the women's singles and
thus raised her total tally of
Wimbledon championship titles
to nineteen, a record previously
held only by Elizabeth Ryan.
Perhaps Miss Ryan's record was
the more amazing, however,
since her titles were all gained in
the two doubles events.

So to the 1976 championship
with the singles going to
Sweden's Björn Borg and to
Chris Evert. The Wimbledon
crowds have always been
recognized as the most
knowledgeable in the world.
They had also remained the
most etiquette conscious of
spectators until the arrival of Ilie
Năstase a few years earlier. A
magnetic personality and
brilliantly talented player,
Năstase attracted young
schoolgirls like a magnet, iron
filings. Yet strong as his appeal
might have been, it was still
nothing compared with that
exercised by the blonde, serious,
yet dynamic young Swede.
Such were the pressures created

by the screaming, squealing teenagers that he needed a police escort to get him to and from the courts on which he played. In 1976 he found accommodation in a secret spot along with Argentinian Guillermo Vilas and practised the week before Wimbledon at a then undisclosed club in north-west London. Perhaps because of his seeming disregard for their attentions, his fans were not quite so prolific or vociferous as in previous years. But of all the modern features of Wimbledon none is more remarkable than the arrival of the teenybopper era, thanks to the magnetism of Năstase and Borg.

And what of the future? For close on 100 years the play has been supreme, but now perhaps the personalities are slowly taking over the game. In thinking about Wimbledon I always recall the words of the late Herman David, the man who led Wimbledon, the Lawn Tennis Association, and the world into the honesty of open tennis. Discussing the championships with me one day, he said, 'I look upon Wimbledon as a beautiful frame into which we put the world's finest pictures each year.' I cannot think of any better way of expressing a policy which has succeeded magnificently for 100 years.

87
Arthur Ashe, the first Black man to win the men's singles. His triumph in 1975 came seventeen years after Althea Gibson's but they had the same coach.

88
Ilie Năstase, the tempestuous, talented and artistic Rumanian, down and on his way out to Sherwood Stewart in 1975

89
Chris Evert, a tennis millionaire by the age of twenty-two. She won Wimbledon in 1974 and 1976.

90
Björn Borg left school at fifteen and promised to win $1 million before he was twenty-one. He did, winning Wimbledon in 1976 on the way.

Championship Personalities

91
Twins Ernest and William Renshaw contesting the 1882 final. They introduced the power game to tennis and enjoyed great popularity.

92
Reggie and Laurie Doherty

Thousands of squealing school-children hustling around Björn Borg may seem a far cry from the quiet dignity of the 200 spectators who saw Spencer Gore win the first Wimbledon championship but there is a strong connecting link between Borg and that first champion. That connecting link is the inner humility of these men and women who have become great champions; in tennis terms, it may be translated as a willingness to learn.

In the case of **Spencer Gore** the willingness to learn was evidenced when he decided that playing against an opponent the other side of a net would be more challenging than hitting the ball against a wall. He took lessons in Real Tennis and these stood him in good stead when the first Wimbledon championship was

staged in 1877. Discovering that the net was 5 feet high at each side-post, he realized that this would handicap shots hit straight down the line and so he seized every opportunity of rushing to the net to end the rallies with devastating volleys. So much for the popular myth that the first Wimbledon championship was a pat-ball affair.

Gore's role as the first great personality was taken over by the **Renshaw Twins**, William and Ernest. Though slightly on the frail side, they introduced into tennis the all-court power game which is commonplace today. Ernest had the purer style but William had slightly more aggression and it was this that cost him the title in 1887. So consistently did his desperate opponents lob against his bewildering and net-rushing tactics that he developed severe tennis-elbow from continually killing the ball and was forced to retire. His name appears on the singles' trophy seven times, a record which to this day has never been surpassed.

The Renshaws were succeeded by the **Doherty Brothers**, Laurence and Reginald, the outstanding players between the years 1897 and 1906. They would probably have dominated even longer but their mother feared for their health and persuaded them to retire. Her fears were justified when Laurie died at the age of forty-three, after Reginald when only thirty-six.

Wonderfully stylish in their stroke play, they were glittering personalities and wonderful sportsmen who were sought as houseguests not only by all the prominent families in England but all over Europe as well. Laurie won the Wimbledon singles five times and Reginald four times, their only setback coming in 1901 when Arthur Wentworth Gore defeated Reginald for the singles title. Gore was to make history in 1909 when, aged forty-one, he beat M.J.G. Ritchie in the final, thus becoming the oldest champion. He retains this record after 100 years of Wimbledon.

93
Björn Borg's teeny bopper fans in 1974 and 1975 forced the committee to engage police escorts.

93
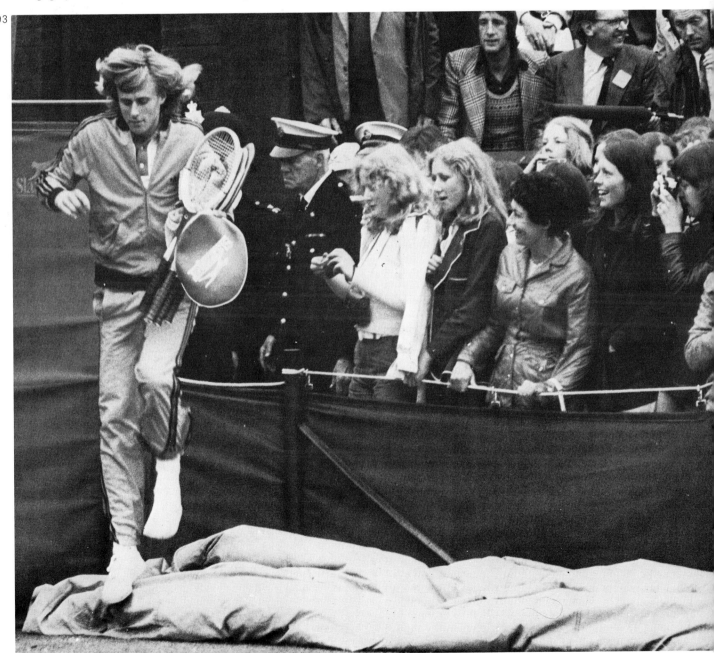

94

'Big Bill' Tilden. Losing the top of a finger forced him to modify his game and he then became as great a personality as he was a player.

95

Anthony Wilding, New Zealand, everybody's ideal as a popular hero. He lost his life in World War I.

94

95

Norman Brookes, a tall, rangy Australian who featured a cloth cap and a devastatingly deceptive left-handed service, became the first overseas outright champion – excluding Irishmen – when he defeated Gore in the 1907 final. An attractive, aggressive player, Brookes made a strong impression on the game but nothing like so strong as he was to make forty years later as Sir Norman Brookes, president of the Australian Tennis Association. His skill as an administrator played a major part in Australia's 20-year domination of post-war international tennis.

In his turn Brookes was succeeded by **Anthony Wilding**, a handsome, daring New Zealander who won his country's

championship at the age of seventeen before coming to England to study at Cambridge University. Wilding was a spectacular figure whether on court or riding his powerful motorcycle. That motorcycle carried him to tournaments all over the continent and was visible evidence of his great sense of adventure. He lost his title to Brookes in 1914, was one of the first men to volunteer for active service, and was tragically killed in Belgium during May 1915.

World War I halted tennis in Britain but not in the USA, where a 6-foot 3-inch, lean and athletic **William Tatem Tilden** was developing both the strokes and tactical knowledge which, allied to his theatrical personality, were to make him probably the

greatest player in the history of the game. A frustrated actor, he did make one appearance on the New York stage and he tried his hand at playwriting but with little success. So this trait in his personality came over strongly on the tennis courts. Yet when his reign came to an end with a defeat by René Lacoste of France in 1927 he showed that his sportsmanship was every bit the equal of all his other character-istics in the gracious way in which he accepted his situation and praised the skill of Lacoste.

René Lacoste was one of four great Frenchmen who dominated tennis for a six-year period in the 1920s. The others were **Henri Cochet, Jacques 'Toto' Brugnon**, and the irrepressible 'bounding Basque', **Jean**

96
Jean Borotra, champion in 1924
and 1926. A typical French stage
'gallant', his vivid personality and
insatiable drive were irresistible.

97
René Lacoste, the great brain of
tennis, on and off court. He
invented and pioneered modern
metal rackets. Champion in 1925
and 1928.

98
Jacques Brugnon (left) and Henri
Cochet

Borotra. Lacoste, Cochet, and
Borotra each won Wimbledon
on two occasions, and their
strength added to that of
Brugnon enabled them to hold
on to the Davis Cup for the six
years from 1927 to 1932, Britain
ending their run in the 1933 final.
Borotra remains a great
Wimbledon figure even to this
day, his participation in the
veteran event giving him the
unparalleled record of competing
at Wimbledon for over fifty
years. Lacoste's work can be seen
on any court at Wimbledon
during the fortnight in the shape
of the Wilson all-metal tennis
rackets of which he was the
inventor and is still the patent
holder. All four of those four
musketeers, as they were known,
still take a prominent part in

French tennis though Brugnon is now in his eighties and the others are all in their seventies.

Their reign was ended by the only truly great British player since World War I, **Frederick John Perry**. Perry started a minor revolution in British tennis for until his domination of the British game the top players had all come from what was considered the 'upper crust' of British society. Perry came from the 'wrong side of the tracks' but his success started the democratization of British tennis. Today tens of thousands of youngsters from the so-called working classes play eagerly and enthusiastically each year, thanks to coaching schemes staged by sponsors and county associations. A flamboyant character, Perry's thoroughness may be perceived in one simple example. He used to watch the Centre Court being cut each day, carefully noting in which direction the cutter travelled. Then, later in the day, when hard-up for a point he would direct one of his drives along a track with the nap of the cut, so gaining an extra foot or two of speed. Perry's period as the top amateur came to an end only when he signed to play Ellsworth Vines in a series of professional matches.

He was succeeded by Californian **Donald Budge**, the son of a former Glasgow Rangers footballer. Those who do not consider Tilden the greatest player in history usually name Budge for that honour, though he is closely challenged by Rod Laver. Budge brought power tennis as near to perfection as possible. Winning all three events at Wimbledon in 1937, he repeated the feat in 1938. In winning the singles that year he did not concede even one set. Then he, too, joined Tilden, Vines, and Perry in the professional ranks. He earned approximately $150,000 in his first year and on it he paid a little over $2,000 in income tax. Allowing for inflation and increased taxation, he reckoned at the start of 1977 that he would today need to earn around $800,000 to be equally well off. Naturally he does not consider he was forty years too early.

Thus Budge left the field wide open to fellow American **Robert Larrimore Riggs**, who also won all three events, on his first appearance in 1939. World War II restricted Riggs's career but he was a great gamester who became even more famous in the middle 1970s with the most outrageous challenge matches. These included one against Billie Jean King which attracted the biggest crowd in tennis history: over 30,000.

The end of World War II saw a period of American dominance led by **Jack Kramer**, one of the most thorough champions of them all and certainly the most underrated. Arguably number four in any list of all-time greats, he won Wimbledon in 1947, followed that up by taking the American championship, and then turned professional. His influence on Wimbledon extends to this day for not only did he turn the then disorganized and unreliable professional game into one of some dignity but later he helped form the Association of Tennis Professionals and is now their executive director. His voice is well-known to British television viewers through his intelligent and perceptive commentaries on the Wimbledon championships each year.

A sunny Australian, **Frank Sedgman**, began a long Australian pre-eminence at Wimbledon by taking the singles in 1952. Tremendously quick and a great competitor, his happy appearance on court brought joy to many. It also inspired enormous numbers of Australians to aim for championship levels, and his win in 1952 was followed in 1956 and 1957 by superb tennis from Lewis Hoad who beat Ken Rosewall in the 1956 final and Ashley Cooper one year later.

99
Don Budge and Alice Marble. Their power won the mixed doubles in 1937 and 1938, when opponents said it was like playing two men.

100
Sunny Frank Sedgman, Australia, the 1952 champion. Viscount Templewood watches Princess Marina present the cup.

101
Jack Kramer won in 1947, then took the USA title and went professional. He turned chaos into order and respectability in the professional game. Such is his prestige that his endorsed racket is still the top seller in the USA.

101

But who of those who visited Wimbledon in the early 1950s can ever forget those golden teenagers, **Lew Hoad** and **Ken Rosewall**? Hoad's amateur career ended in 1957 when he turned professional. Rosewall, who had been runner-up in the singles in 1954, was to repeat that limited success on three more occasions, the last of them in 1974. No other man has ever stayed at the top for even half that period of time. Hoad was the exponent of power, Rosewall of sheer technical perfection, backed by exceptional quickness and tremendous tactical skill.

One other great who never won Wimbledon, yet who made a tremendous impression on spectators is **Pancho Gonzales**. He figured in the longest single ever played there when he beat Charles Pasarell in a 112-game, 5-set battle which spread itself over two days in the year 1969. Begun late in the day, the first set went to Pasarell 24-22, despite constant appeals by the angry Gonzales that the light was inadequate for play. His pleas were ignored by the referee, Captain Mike Gibson, and Pasarell went on to win the second set 6-1 with Gonzales' angry gestures and demonstrations being relayed to millions of viewers via British television. Play was finally stopped and long before 2 o'clock on the next afternoon the queue for admission stretched for a greater distance than ever before in the history of Wimbledon. Those who stood in that queue must have had second sight for the next three sets, all of which were won by Gonzales, contained some of the greatest drama ever seen on the Centre Court. Pasarell held seven match points but was unable to win one.

102
Ken Rosewall (left) and Lew Hoad, teenage, wonder-boy winners of the doubles in 1953

103
Rod Laver, the best Australian player in tennis history

102   103

104

104
Pancho Gonzales. The 'amateurs only' rule kept him out of Wimbledon from 1949 to 1968 but he still made a gigantic impression when he returned.

105
Jimmy Connors lost to Arthur Ashe in the 1975 final at a time when he was suing Ashe for $2 million for libel.

105

Returning to the champions, **Rod Laver** took the title in 1961 and 1962 and completed a grand slam before turning professional. The advent of open tennis in 1968 enabled him to win the singles on two further occasions and also to complete open tennis's first grand slam of the world's four major singles titles, so becoming the first man to achieve this impressive feat. A redheaded left-hander, so great was his love of the game when a child that he built himself his own practice wall and hit against it until he was good enough to be allowed to join his parents and brother in the regular weekend games on their court in the garden.

Laver's position as the world number one came to an end when **Jimmy Connors** took the singles title in 1974. Coached at first by his grandmother and mother, they soon decided he needed more advanced assistance and so the family moved to Los Angeles, where Jimmy came strongly under the influence of Pancho Segura and Bill Riordan, the latter a business manager and wily promoter cum tennis politician. Under Riordan's guidance, Connors sued numerous organizations for millions of dollars under the American anti-trust laws. Brash, eager and immensely talented, Connors seemed destined to top the world rankings for many years but lurking in the background was a man with different ideas, Arthur Ashe. The 1975 singles final against Ashe meant meeting the man Connors was suing for $2 million, surely a unique final in any field of sport.

55

106
Arthur Ashe showing the athleticism
needed to become champion

107
Björn Borg. Even when on his
knees, he still fights to keep going.

108
Miss Maud Watson

109
Lottie Dod when fifteen years old

108

Miss L. Dod,
Winner of the Ladies Championship.

109

An intelligent, articulate Black American, **Arthur Ashe** set himself the target of winning both the WCT title in Dallas and the Wimbledon singles in 1975. His dignity and persuasiveness as president of ATP evidenced his administrative talents and he brought this organizational strength to bear on the task of overthrowing Connors. Wimbledon's fast Centre Court puts a premium on power. But Ashe beat Connors with a superb mixture of softly hit, well-placed 'junk' and judicious switches to aggression whenever Connors looked like mastering the slower tactics.

So to **Björn Borg** who, with Ilie Năstase, the brilliant, artistic, temperamental Rumanian, brought into tennis the cult of pop idolatry with its thousands of screaming, teeny-bopper schoolgirls frantically helter-skeltering hither and thither. If the first image of Wimbledon is of the 200 well-behaved, polite onlookers watching an old

Harrovian win the championship, the latest must surely be of high heels digging up the Centre Court when screaming teenagers raced across it for Borg's autograph. Yet, such is Wimbledon's ability to surmount all hazards, that the committee showed no greater outward concern than their predecessors in 1886, when they found a daisy on the Centre Court; they coped, quietly.

Women first played in the Wimbledon championships back in 1884, when **Maud Watson** defeated her sister Lillian in the final. Like so many of her successors, Maud Watson was a determined young lady and she had developed her game practising against young men who came to study with her father at Cambridge.

Until the 1920s, women were always somewhat handicapped by the clothes they wore. But in 1887 **Charlotte 'Lottie' Dod** broke with tradition by wearing skirts that ended at least 9 inches

from the ground. A born athlete, she became the youngest ever champion by taking the women's singles that year. She won again in 1888, 1891, 1892, and 1893 before quitting the game out of boredom. Though women were gentle creatures in those days, Lottie advocated all-out aggression and was a formidable net player. But, strangely, she persisted with an underarm service right through to the end of her playing career.

Her record of five wins was equalled by Charlotte Cooper, later **Mrs Alfred Sterry**, but in 1903 one of the eternal names in the world game took the title for the first time, Dorothea Douglass (later **Mrs Lambert Chambers**). She won the singles seven times in all and in 1919 was twice within a point of an eighth victory against the immortal Suzanne Lenglen. (The record of the greatest number of wins in the women's singles is in fact held by Helen Wills Moody, who won eight times in all.)

110
Mrs Alfred Sterry, née 'Chattie'
Cooper, one of the most beautiful
of Wimbledon's champions

110

111

111
Mrs Lambert Chambers, the greatest
British woman player in Wimbledon's
100 years

112
Suzanne Lenglen brought the art
and grace of ballet, for which she
trained, into tennis.

112

Dorothea Douglass was an extremely determined young woman who had learned her tennis in what is still a hot-bed of enthusiasm for the game, Ealing in Middlesex. She too practised frequently against men and so developed one of the best forehand drives in the history of tennis. A wonderful sports-woman, she remained in the top class from 1903 until 1925. In that year she won both her singles and a doubles in the Wightman Cup match against America and so at the age of forty-seven ended the year ranked number seven in the world, truly a phenomenal performance.

If Mrs Lambert Chambers was noted for her power and tenacity, then **Suzanne Lenglen** was to become immortal through her immense flair and striking personality. She, along with Bill Tilden among the men, undoubtedly started the cult of personality, in which players of the game became more famous than the game itself, except at Wimbledon. Suzanne was beaten just once between the years 1909 and 1925, and then only because she played within twenty-four hours of completing a transatlantic sea-crossing and when she was scarcely fit. Volatile and temperamental, she never forgave the woman who beat her, Molla Mallory, and at Wimbledon some years later she thrashed that Norwegian turned American in the shortest women's final on record.

Suzanne's reign was threatened by a beautiful Californian, Helen Wills, later **Helen Wills Moody**, who also gained some fame as a watercolourist. Helen and Suzanne met only once in competition, in the South of France where Suzanne won narrowly in two sets. Helen, less mobile than the majority of players of her day, hit with tremendous power and had immense powers of anticipation, concentration, and determination. Possibly one of the first women tennis players to employ psychological systems, she went to bed each night saying to herself over and over again, 'I can and I will. I can and I will.' And, my goodness, she did. Her series of eight wins stretched from 1927 to 1938, during which time she was challenged quite strongly by Kitty McKane (later **Mrs Leslie Godfree**), who won in 1924, beating Helen in the final, and then again in 1926. Still an active player though nearing her eighties, she is an avid follower of the game and is to be seen in the members' stand at Wimbledon on most of the days each year. Also a magnificent badminton player, Mrs Godfree was the first woman player to adopt the serve and run to the net tactics brought to perfection in later years by Billie Jean King.

113

114

MISS HELEN WILLS, THE LAWN-TENNIS CHAMPION, DRAWN BY HERSELF: A PICTURE FROM HER ONE-WOMAN EXHIBITION.

113
Kitty McKane, later Mrs Leslie Godfree, twice champion

114
Helen Wills Moody, eight times champion

116

115

118

117

115
Twice champion Dorothy Round

116
Helen Jacobs, champion in 1936

117
Louise Brough, four times singles champion

118
Doris Hart. She overcame a severe leg injury to become a great stylist and champion.

Britain's other pre-war winner of the singles was **Dorothy Round**, a Dudley girl of great principle. Earlier in her career she taught at Sunday school and caused consternation in the French championships by refusing to play on a Sunday. No such problem existed at Wimbledon. Regular practice with Ryuko Miki, a Japanese star with whom she won the mixed doubles, honed Miss Round's strokes to ultra-sharp keenness and it was

this which enabled her to overcome all opposition in 1934 and again in 1937. She too remains active in the game, both as an official of the Worcestershire Lawn Tennis Association and a tennis correspondent with the *Sunday Express*.

Helen Wills Moody's reign during pre-war years was also challenged by Helen Jacobs, ironically from the same city in the United States, San Francisco, and a member of the

same club. Yet despite this a feud
seemed to exist between them
which brought no credit to Mrs
Wills Moody.

Helen Jacobs' persistence and
determination took her to the
final in 1929, 1932, 1934, and
1935, before she finally gained a
reward for her tenacity by
winning the singles in 1936. She
should have won again in 1938
when she held match point in
the final against Mrs Wills Moody,
but, foozling an easy shot, she then
went on to lose.

World War II interrupted the
careers of many women who
seemed destined for greatness, but
the end of the war brought to
light four Americans who
overwhelmed all opposition until
1951 when countrywoman
Maureen Connolly flashed like a
comet across the sky for three
years before a serious riding
accident put an end to her
career. Her predecessors were
**Pauline Betz, Margaret
Osborne, Louise Brough**, and
Doris Hart. All in their different
ways made outstanding
contributions to the game. And
to this day Miss Brough's record
of winning eight events out of
nine in the three years from 1948
to 1950 stands supreme.

Maureen Connolly became
the second youngest winner of
the title in 1952 when she
overthrew Miss Brough. Small
and compact, she hit with a
tremendous power which she
developed through more
intensive practice than any
woman who has yet played at
Wimbledon. Her normal stint
was a minimum of four hours a
day. Her concentration was
enormous and in order to unwind
she would normally go straight
from a tournament win to a
practice court where she could
gradually relax through hitting
the ball smoothly and easily,
rather than with the power and
determination of match play.
Even when she won the
Wimbledon final she followed
this routine, her perfectionist
approach completely overcoming
the natural glee of a seventeen-
year-old girl winning what is
virtually the championship of the
world.

119

120

119
Pauline Betz, champion in 1946 and
now a noted coach

120
Maureen Connolly, singles
champion three times before the
age of twenty

The years 1957 and 1958 belonged to **Althea Gibson**, a Black American who was raised in the toughest quarters of New York. Her autobiography tells of the fist fights she had, some of them with her father, and this aggression showed in her approach to tennis. Always seeking to attack, she had great agility, a wide reach, and remarkable persistence. In contrast, she had a splendid singing voice and she followed an example set by her fellow countrywoman, Alice Marble, back in 1939 by entertaining the 1,000 tennis bigwigs who attended the final Wimbledon ball with songs which she later recorded.

She was succeeded by the only Brazilian who has so far won the women's singles, **Maria Bueno**, surely the most graceful player ever to take the title. She won the singles three times in all, and her grace plus her outstanding flair for making good dresses appear ultra-beautiful has earned her a place among the tennis immortals.

Maria developed a personal rivalry with Margaret Smith, later **Mrs Margaret Court**, who has won more major titles around the world than any other woman in history. A woman of splendid talent, Margaret is a profoundly committed Christian and it was her religious belief which enabled her to overcome the greatest nervousness ever displayed by a player of her standard. No woman has trained harder, and in tests carried out by *The Sunday Times* her strength and suppleness rivalled that of many near top-class male athletes.

A third immortal entered this arena of tennis greats in the person of Billie Jean Moffitt, later to become **Mrs Billie Jean King**. She gave promise of the things to come when in partnership with Karen Hentze she won the women's doubles in 1961. Both were still in their teens. Mrs King went on to become the great leader of the Women's Lib movement in tennis and the founder of that controversial area of the game, world team-tennis. Currently she has won nineteen Wimbledon championships, the total she shares with Elizabeth Ryan. Miss Ryan was present at Wimbledon in 1976, hopeful that Mrs King would beat her own record. 'Records are made to be beaten,' she said. 'I hope Billie Jean beats mine.'

Mrs King's only unexpected setback in the singles came in 1969 when **Ann Jones** of Birmingham finally overcame her reputation of always being the woman who came in second and beat Mrs King in the final. Runner-up in all three events in the table-tennis championships of 1957, she won the French tennis championship in 1961 and again in 1966, but until 1969 it seemed the greatest of them all, Wimbledon, would evade her. At the International Club dinner dance on the eve of Wimbledon she seemed in a happy and relaxed mood which boded well for the coming championship and she retained that relaxation through a tremendous semi-final and then final.

And so to the last in this chain of great champions, **Chris Evert**. Still in her early twenties, her prowess with the racket has already made her a tennis millionaire and twice Wimbledon winner. Yet she has made it clear that she would prefer to be recognized as a 'thoroughly female female', rather than the world's greatest woman tennis player. But this in no way disrupts her intense practice and application to the game. Indeed, like Charlotte Dod back at the end of the nineteenth century, Miss Evert has become slightly bored with the lack of severe opposition. She has talked about retiring at an early age and this is certainly a possibility.

Who could succeed her? Perhaps Britain's Sue Barker, the Paignton princess, or Evonne Goolagong Cawley, who began 1977 in the early throes of pregnancy. Highly talented, Mrs Cawley brings to the game one characteristic that stood out in those pioneering days of the 1880s: joy in playing. Remember that old saying: 'The more things change, the more

121
Althea Gibson. Fist fights in Harlem taught her aggression and toughness.

122
Ann Jones, who won in 1969 and gained the MBE as an additional reward

they stay the same'? Maybe this is coming true in women's tennis.

In discussing the greats, both men and women, it is fashionable to name one's choice as the all-time Wimbledon champion. People claim that in all measurable games irrefutable evidence of consistent progress can be established with times, distances and so on.

To leave readers of this section with an intriguing thought, here is a chain of results which was published in *Lawn Tennis* magazine some years ago, after it had been compiled by Lance Tingay. It provides irrefutable proof that Spencer Gore was greater than Björn Borg. Surely there must be a fallacy in it somewhere?

Here is the chain – it reads like something out of 'Genesis'.

Spencer W. Gore (at Wimbledon 1877 by 6-1, 6-2, 6-4) **beat W. Marshall,**
who (at Wimbledon 1877 by 6-5, 5-6, 6-4, 6-1) **beat L. Erskine,**
who (at Wimbledon 1878 by 6-4, 3-6, 6-1, 3-6, 6-5) **beat W.J. Hamilton,**
who (at Wimbledon 1890 by 0-6, 6-4, 6-4, 6-2) **beat J. Pim,**
who (at Wimbledon 1894 by 10-8, 6-2, 8-6) **beat W. Baddeley,**
who (at Wimbledon 1897 by 6-4, 6-2, 6-2) **beat H.L. Doherty,**
who (in the USA Champs 1903 by 6-0, 6-3, 10-8) **beat W.A. Larned,**
who (in the USA Champs 1911 by 6-4, 6-4, 6-2) **beat M. McLoughlin,**
who (in the USA Champs 1915 by 6-2, 6-4, 6-0) **beat F.T. Hunter,**
who (in the USA Champs 1928 by 7-5, 3-6, 6-3, 6-4) **beat J. Crawford,**
who (in the Australian Champs 1935 by 6-1, 1-6, 6-2, 3-6, 6-3) **beat A.K. Quist,**
who (in the Australian Champs 1947 by 6-3, 6-2, 6-3) **beat F.A. Sedgman,**
who (at Wembley 1960 by 4-6, 6-2, 6-2) **beat A. Olmedo,**
who (at Wimbledon 1959 by 6-4, 6-3, 6-4) **beat R.G. Laver,**
who (in Philadelphia 1970 by 4-6, 6-2, 7-6) **beat I. Năstase,**
who (in the Masters', Boston, 1973 by 6-3, 7-5) **beat J. Connors,**
who (in the USA Open 1976 by 6-4, 3-6, 7-6, 6-4) **beat B. Borg.**

123
Maria Bueno. They named a São Paulo street after her.

124
Chris Evert, the 'ice maiden', melts on winning the 1974 final.

Nineteen years separated Dorothea Lambert Chambers' first, successful finals appearance from the moment she walked on court to meet the French girl whose scintillating tennis and electric personality had already captured British crowds during the 1919 championships.

Headed by the King, Queen and Princess Mary, 8,000 eager fans packed the Centre Court in anticipation of an outstanding final. They were not disappointed. Time may have taken its toll but Mrs Lambert Chambers remained a great, clever and courageous player. Long, testing rallies left her 3–5 down in the first set but she recovered to reach set point at 6–5. Losing this chance and the set, Mrs Lambert Chambers slammed her way through the second.

Swallowing sugar soaked in cognac, Suzanne, white faced, raced to 4–1 in the third. Heroically, Mrs Lambert Chambers fought back and in an electrifying atmosphere reached 6–5 and 40–15. Never flinching, Suzanne hit to the forehand and raced for the net, there to be halted by a lob that looked out of her reach. Leaping back, Suzanne threw up her racket and contacted the ball with the tip of its frame. The ball crawled over the net, catching the champion flat footed and surprised. 'I never saw the ball,' Suzanne confessed later. Thus reprieved, Suzanne again made for the net. The counter shot sped the ball for a wide gap and all seemed over. Alas for British hopes, it hit the net band.

Though the tension and outstanding rallies were maintained to the end, Suzanne was never again in danger of defeat and she went on to win 10–8, 4–6, 9–7. Viewed in retrospect, this was a classic contest. Despite the daring of both players, the errors were negligible and each point was a battle in itself. At the finish, Suzanne's feet were bleeding and both women were so exhausted that it was impossible for them to go to the royal box. At a later date the King told Mrs Lambert Chambers that he felt quite ill from watching, a view echoed by most of those present.

Great Games
Lenglen v Lambert Chambers 1919

125

126

125
Mrs Lambert Chambers. A fluke shot by Suzanne Lenglen cost her the 1919 final and so her eighth singles championship.

126
Suzanne Lenglen, winner in 1919 of the most dramatic women's final in 100 years

Overwhelming power had stamped Ellsworth Vines as the greatest player of the previous year. Memories of his 1932 semi-final left the public no reason to believe that Jack Crawford could avoid a repeat of the thrashing he had then received. But the thoughtful Australian held different ideas. Close study of Vines had revealed one tiny flaw in the champion's seemingly perfect technique and with many hours of meticulous rehearsal

Crawford evolved a system for probing that tiny weakness. There remained the problem of Vines' 128 mph services. Crawford decided to solve this not by retreating but by moving well forward to use his lightning reflexes in blocking back the ball as best he could.

Vines thundered his way confidently through the first set, and nineteen games of the second set went by before Crawford's eyes finally attuned themselves to

the cannonball services sufficiently to obtain a break. Brilliantly attacking Vines' tremendous forehand, Crawford volleyed with great daring and, despite the breathtaking pace of the rallies, unforced errors were rarities.

Slowly Crawford's resistance to his opponent's strength contained Vines, and the end came with Crawford breaking service to win 4-6, 11-9, 6-2, 2-6, and 6-4.

Crawford v Vines 1933

127

128

127
Modest in victory, Ellsworth Vines suffered his 1933 final upset by Jack Crawford, left, with graciousness and supreme sportsmanship.

128
Ellsworth Vines, probably the hardest hitter in tennis history

Drobny v Patty 1953

129

130

The year 1953 belonged to Jaroslav Drobny. Runner-up in 1949 eleven years after his debut and again the losing finalist in 1952, the popular, self-exiled Czech had trained meticulously for a bid to achieve his greatest tennis dream. But luck turned its back. In the third round he met Budge Patty, the 1950 champion and a man with whom he always played long matches. This was to be no exception.

For ninety-three games spread over 4 hours and 20 minutes the two men, both stylists in their own way, traded some of the finest shots seen on the Centre Court since the end of World War II. Patty's goal was the net position. To thwart him, Drobny strove constantly to get there first. Three times in the fourth set and thrice in the fifth only one point separated Patty from victory. Six times Drobny smiled wanly at his wife high in the crowd before unleashing breathtaking plays. As dusk turned to near darkness, the digits on the electric scoreboard shone out like so many search-lights. Neither man faltered. At last Drobny reached match point. Pausing momentarily, he took his chance and 15,000 wildly cheering spectators sustained their unremitting, noisy praise for 5 unforgettable minutes. The final score was 8-6, 16-18, 3-6, 8-6, 12-10.

Yet ultimately the effort was in vain for it had broken a blood vessel in Drobny's leg. He survived two more rounds but could scarcely move while losing the semi-final.

129
Jaroslav Drobny wearily rising after a fall during his epic with Budge Patty in 1953. Wimbledon gave each man a special memento of this great contest of skill and stamina.

130
Patty takes a shot to his backhand.

American tennis in the 1940s and 1950s clung hard to the middle- and upper-class customs it had known since the arrival of the game there in the 1880s.

This was no place for a Black girl, especially one raised on the 'wrong side of the tracks'. So the fight to become a somebody in tennis had proved arduous and long for Althea Gibson. Tall and gangling, she was a fine natural athlete but not the easiest of characters. Overcoming all obstacles, she won the French championship in 1956 but faltered at Wimbledon. In 1957, gaining in confidence, she reached the final where her opponent was her doubles partner, Darlene Hard, an experienced campaigner. Much was expected of Miss Gibson but past occasions were dotted with unexpected let-downs and she was now less than two months short of her thirtieth birthday.

Her opponent across the net had also come up the rough way, working as a waitress to save money for her tennis career. She, too, was geared up for a supreme effort to fulfil a dream and open the gate to financial security. The expected epic never even started. For once sustaining her full capabilities from first to last point, Miss Gibson overwhelmed Miss Hard 6-3, 6-2, so to write a new page of tennis history by becoming the first Black to win a Wimbledon singles.

Gibson v Hard 1957

131

132

131
Attack is the best way to overcome an attacking opponent so Althea Gibson is volleying at the net.

132
Victory and Darlene Hard's congratulations after the 1957 final

Mortimer v Truman 1961

It was 1961 and the first all-British women's singles final since Mrs Lambert Chambers and Mrs Larcombe had fought it out forty-seven years earlier: Angela Mortimer, the shy, retiring but ultra-determined Devonian from Plymouth, everybody's dream of the ideal girl next door, and Christine Truman from Woodford, well beloved by British crowds.

Defeat seemed near for Angela Mortimer when she scraped back a simple return which should have given Christine Truman a 6-4, 5-3 lead. But the ball tipped the net and bumped slightly off course. Moving quickly to complete a coup, Christine slipped, fell and clasped her leg in agony.

Minutes crawled by before she slowly hobbled back to restart play. Pouncing like some avenging eagle, Angela swept the ball remorselessly from side to side to grasp her 15-year-old dream. What of the crowd? 'Christine can have the sympathy,' said the triumphant Miss Mortimer, Britain's first champion since 1937. 'I've got the cup.'

133
Angela Mortimer and Christine Truman after the all-British 1961 final

134
Christine Truman is made to stretch.

135
Determination on the face of champion-to-be Angela Mortimer

134

135

Jones v King 1969

As she danced with a friend at the eve of Wimbledon ball in 1969 Ann Jones seemed unusually composed and happy. Was this finally her Wimbledon? The draw indicated 'no' – Margaret Court was in her half and Mrs King looked certain to come through the other half. And indeed she did but Mrs Jones exceeded her best in beating Mrs Court to earn a repeat of the 1967 final.

It seemed she hadn't a chance. Mrs King knew a formula for overwhelming Mrs Jones' backhand and when she raced through the first set 6–3 it looked like another telling of the same old story. But Mrs Jones thought otherwise. Instead of defending, she seized the attack by beating Mrs King to the net, there to volley with brave audacity and telling certainty. Nonplussed by this change of tactic and disgruntled by the crowd's partisanship, Mrs King could find no effective answers. Mrs Jones, confidence growing with every point won, sailed forward to victory 3–6, 6–3, 6–2.

136

136
Beaten and disappointed, Billie Jean King still hastens to congratulate 1969 champion Ann Jones.

137
Billie Jean attacks . . .

138
. . . and Ann Jones defends during the 1969 final.

137

138

Gonzales v Pasarell 1969

A living tennis legend, Pancho Gonzales was lost to Wimbledon for eighteen years before the championship was opened to professionals in 1968. Some years past his best, Gonzales, aged forty-one, began his 1969 first-round match against Charles Pasarell late on the opening day. Pasarell, then twenty-five, had sensationally eliminated the top seed in the first round two years earlier. The odds seemed heavily stacked against Gonzales.

As the first set stretched its way, 5 all, 6 all, on to 22 all, the daylight faded and with it Gonzales' ability to see the ball. Repeatedly he complained . . . and harangued a gaggle of persecuters among the by now 'full house' Centre Court crowd. Referee Captain Mike Gibson

139
Pancho Gonzales

140
Charles Pasarell

141
The irresistible force

142
The immovable object

came to the court, ordered that play be continued and sat down to watch. Furious, Gonzales kept on assailing him with angry words and glowerings, all plainly seen in close up as television cameras zoomed down to capture every angry gesture. Completely impervious, Gonzales maintained a running battle until Pasarell took a two sets to nil lead and Gibson finally gave the 'no more play' sign.

Storming off court amid boos, Gonzales could scarcely have dreamed what the next day would bring. They had already played fifty-three games, and there were fifty-nine more to come before the tigerish teacher had saved seven match points and finally overcome his former pupil. No words can capture the primitive aggression with which the invincible Gonzales tore victory from Pasarell's grip, took the lead for the first time after 111 games and then ended this unforgettable epic 22-24, 1-6, 16-14, 6-3, 11-9. Gonzales has always prayed on court. It seemed he was answered that day.

141

142

Court v King 1970

Tennis is littered with personality clashes among its stars and the vibrations could be felt in the stands when Margaret Court and Billie Jean King began their final in the 1970 championships.

Champion in 1966, 1967, and 1968, Mrs King was determined to regain the crown she had lost to Mrs Jones in 1969. Mrs Court, twice champion, was no less determined to assert her superiority. Neither was in any mood to compromise and from the very first point the pattern of each woman's play was clear: attack at all costs.

Mrs King led 3-2, 5-4, 7-6 and 8-7 in the first set, but, no matter how tenaciously she fought to clinch it, Mrs Court still swept over her. Apparent attacks evoked no show of sympathy and Mrs Court took the set 11-9. Ahead 1-0 in the second set, Mrs King trailed thereafter. She tried varying her game but to no avail. The rallies continued at an awesome pace but with the Australian woman's greater strength becoming ever more valuable. Mrs King resisted for 147 minutes and staved off five match points but could not prevent Mrs Court winning the 'most games ever' women's final 14-12, 11-9.

143

143
The end of a wonderful final. Margaret Court beats Billie Jean King.

144
Margaret Court. Prayers and courage gave her strength.

144

145
All-out aggression in the 1972 final
between Ilie Năstase and Stan
Smith (near end)

146
Smith consoles disconsolate loser
Năstase and amuses the Sunday
crowd.

146

Smith v Năstase 1972

Ilie Năstase's flamboyant personality, mercurial temperament and bewildering, natural talent; Stan Smith's immense 6 foot 4 inch height, mighty power and solid Christian virtue. What more exciting mix could have been poured into the Centre Court for the 1972 final?

While rain poured down throughout Saturday they waited in vain to start. When the final began on Sunday Năstase soon showed signs of tension. For two sets he angrily banged his racket strings and harangued the supplier in the stands. His gestures only encouraged the calmly determined Smith. And it was a psychological advantage Smith needed, for when Năstase concentrated on play his dazzling shots and cat-like mobility threatened to run away with victory.

Smith had used yoga in his pre-Wimbledon training and the stretching exercises he learned proved invaluable when, attacking in the only way he knew, he dived hither and thither in reaching Năstase's whiplash drives and passing shots.

The fiery Rumanian looked superior as the fifth set wore on and several crucial Smith saves shrieked of luck – or answered prayers? But courageous solidity finally destroyed artistic sensitivity: 4-6, 6-3, 6-3, 4-6, 7-5.

Ashe v Connors 1975

No-one could overthrow the holder, Jimmy Connors, or so the betting-shop wagers suggested. But those who placed such bets knew little of the scheming skills of Arthur Ashe, that calm disciple of Dr Walter Johnson, the black physician who guided Althea Gibson to the Wimbledon title.

Ashe undertook a thorough, analytical study of Connors' famous technique and began the final with a plan: to feed Connors with a mixture of varied, mostly soft, 'junk', majoring on low, spinning, short-angled skidders to Connors' main strength, his double-handed backhand.

The plan worked perfectly. Except in the third set and for three games in the fourth, Connors never slipped free of the clever shackles used by Ashe. So he dumbfounded all but a few to become the first Black and probably cleverest ever men's singles champion 6-1, 6-1, 5-7, 6-4.

147
Defending champion Jimmy Connors tries to attack.

148
An anguished Ashe lobs short.

149
Half a minute's meditation works wonders for Ashe's calmness.

148

Fashion at the Championships

CONTEST FOR THE LADIES' CHAMPIONSHIP AT WIMBLEDON.

150
Miss M.E. Robb. Tight corsets or not, there goes a mighty service.

151
Line meant more than lissomness to the lady competitors of 1886.

153

154

152
The daring, ankle-showing dress of the 1907 champion, May Sutton of the USA.

153
The 'shocking' knee-length stockings and lacy slip of Suzanne Lenglen

155

154
Helen Wills Moody made eye-shades a must back in the 1920s.

155
Dorothy Round (right) and Helen Jacobs before their 1934 final. Tailored, long culottes were then the rage.

Tennis took off on the day Major Wingfield introduced his concept of an amalgam of several games during a house party at Nantclwyd. He named it 'Sphairistike' and, like the lavish clothes worn by the ladies who tremulously tried their hands that day, survival of this clumsy name was short lived.

The tightly corsetted, waspish line persisted but by the 1880s all-white outfits had become *de rigueur* for ambitious women players, at least at Wimbledon. The 'predominantly white' rule

156
Lea Pericoli, Italy, a frothy blend of lace and decoration in the colourful 1950s

157
Virginia Wade in 1975. She keeps Britain high in the fashion stakes.

158
With prize money increasing by the 1970s, women's wear grew more functional, as this dress worn by Françoise Durr of France shows clearly.

159
Trim, well-fitting mini-dresses enhance Chris Evert's appeal and give her ease of movement for her unsuccessful 1975 title bid.

156 has to a large extent applied throughout the ninety-three years since 1884 when Maud Watson's elegant, long-sleeved white dress was topped by a snazzy, abbreviated white 'boater' and tailed by soft and shapeless white ankle-boots. There was nothing to compare with the two American girls who were scheduled to attend a party after playing their USA doubles championship semi-final so to save time wore their party dresses for the match.

Lottie Dod, the fifteen-year-old winner in 1887, swapped the traditional dressy, pretty hat for something approximating to the flat, peaked caps popular with many of to-day's model girls. She also hoisted her skirts to calf length to help her scuttle around the court . . . still wearing those ghastly, if fashionable, boots of the day.

The game slowly became more important than excessive fashion. The hour-glass slowly straightened, white plimsolls replaced boots, and in 1905 down-to-earth May Sutton rolled up her sleeves during her successful bid to capture the title for the USA. Not until 1926 when South African Bobbie Tapscott came on to the Centre Court stockingless was public so outraged. 'That is how I played on our farm back home,' she wrote later. 'I never dreamed it would cause such a sensation.'

Despite the daring of Lottie Dod, skirts remained close to the ground right up to 1914. Hats slowly disappeared but although a freer line in dresses was developing, corsets were still worn and one of the less pleasant sights in the ladies' changing room was the rail for hanging these ugly, often bloodstained, garments out to dry. How the women of those days ran so fleetly when steel and bone were lacerating their bodies defies imagination. It also measures the high degree of motivation of the then supposedly weaker sex.

World War I changed many things, including attitudes to women in sport. Suzanne Lenglen spearheaded the slow-growing attack on crippling tradition. She made her debut in a one-piece, cotton dress that reached only to her calves. Petticoat and corset she traded for greater mobility and, horrors, short sleeves bared her elbows for all to see.

A balletomane, her attitude was governed by that art. As success and confidence increased, so the style of her clothing grew bolder. Her knee-length, shiny stockings and the ample expanses of leg and thigh exposed by her frequent, graceful, mighty leaps brought forth cries of 'disgraceful' and 'indecent', fortunately swamped by her brilliant playing skills. Suzanne unquestionably liberated women from their traditional outer garments. Shorts were introduced by Grace Tomblin in the mid-1930s, though it was the talented Helen Jacobs who emphasized that practicality outweighed notoriety by wearing shorts on the Centre Court.

The craving for colour expressed itself in the wearing of matching cardigans by many doubles pairs. Underclothes were worn for cover rather than effect. This changed in the 1950s when Gussie Moran treated the Centre Court males to an abundance of lace-trimmed knickers that had many an eager photographer flat on the ground in search of better

158

159

pictures. Exposure, both for greater mobility and camera catching, ever increases and who can deny the joy in watching a beautifully bronzed, shapely young woman on court?

Maria Bueno brought an imperiousness to tennis which designer Teddy Tinling sought to enhance with colour. Restricted to white on the outer side of garments, he began lining his creations with gorgeous purples and other complementing hues. Coloured trims grew in popularity. Flowered patterns took over but always there were the eagle-eyed committee members to censor all but the smallest hints of the gorgeous tints evolved by modern technology. Even in the 'liberated' 1970s Rosemary Casals was sent from Court No. 1 to change the highly coloured outfit in which she aimed to play. Pre-court inspections now abound . . . and not just for the women. Don't imagine that men are new to the colour game. Long ago in the

160
Arthur Ashe in 1975, the year men became conscious of cut and colour in their dress

160

161
Raul Ramirez. Small advertising emblems were almost part of a uniform by 1975.

161

1920s, America's John Hennessy was made to change out of the striped trousers in which he proposed to enthrall the Centre Court crowd.

Identifying manufacturers' emblems are the latest cause for pre-court scrutiny. When an 'endorsement' is costing $50,000 or more a year, a profit-conscious manufacturer must ensure that the public are in no doubt about the outfit which makes the star so glamorous. Regulations restrict these emblems to a few square inches but methinks centenary year may pose some wicked problems.

Whispers are of a modish headband worn by Björn Borg and carrying the message 'T.U. BORG'. Advertising? Oh, no. T.U., they say, is the Swedish abbreviation for 'good luck' and who can possibly prohibit the reigning champion wearing such a well-wishing accessory? For sure, all the shrewdest scheming is not confined to that Centre Court.

163
Ken Rosewall. His advertising emblem conforms to the size limitations imposed by the Wimbledon committee.

163

164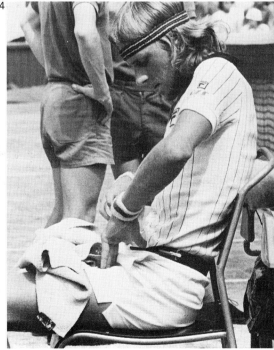

162

162
Zenzo Shimidzu, the first world-class Japanese player, in the long pants worn by male players until World War II.

164
Abundance for Borg. He 'endorses' a racket maker, a brewery with his hair band, an Italian maker of tennis clothes, and someone else's shoes. Gross fees top $100,000 per year.

Records

Until the year 1922 the winners of the singles and the men's doubles championships were not required to play through the preliminary rounds. They were challenged for the championship by the winner of the All-Comers' final. Winners are set in **bold type**.

Men's Singles	Year	Final	Challenge Round
	1877	**S.W. Gore** v W.C. Marshall 6-1, 6-2, 6-4	
	1878	**P.F. Hadow** v L. Erskine 6-4, 6-4, 6-4	**P.F. Hadow** v S.W. Gore 7-5, 6-1, 9-7
	1879	**J.T. Hartley** v V. 'St Leger' Gould 6-2, 6-4, 6-2	**J.T. Hartley**: a bye P.F. Hadow retired
	1880	**H.F. Lawford** v O.E. Woodhouse 7-5, 6-4, 6-0	**J.T. Hartley** v H.F. Lawford 6-0, 6-2, 2-6, 6-3
	1881	**W. Renshaw** v R.T. Richardson 6-4, 6-2, 6-3	**W. Renshaw** v J.T. Hartley 6-0, 6-2, 6-1
	1882	**E. Renshaw** v R.T. Richardson 7-5, 6-2, 2-6, 6-3	**W. Renshaw** v E. Renshaw 6-1, 2-6, 4-6, 6-2, 6-2
	1883	**E. Renshaw** v D. Stewart 0-6, 6-3, 6-0, 6-2	**W. Renshaw** v E. Renshaw 2-6, 6-3, 6-3, 4-6, 6-3
	1884	**H.F. Lawford** v C.W. Grinstead 7-5, 2-6, 6-2, 9-7	**W. Renshaw** v H.F. Lawford 6-0, 6-4, 9-7
	1885	**H.F. Lawford** v E. Renshaw 5-7, 6-1, 0-6, 6-2, 6-4	**W. Renshaw** v H.F. Lawford 7-5, 6-2, 4-6, 7-5
	1886	**H.F. Lawford** v E.W. Lewis 6-2, 6-3, 2-6, 4-6, 6-4	**W. Renshaw** v H.F. Lawford 6-0, 5-7, 6-3, 6-4
	1887	**H.F. Lawford** v E. Renshaw 1-6, 6-3, 3-6, 6-4, 6-4	**H.F. Lawford**: a bye W. Renshaw retired
	1888	**E. Renshaw** v E.W. Lewis 7-9, 6-1, 8-6, 6-4	**E. Renshaw** v H.F. Lawford 6-3, 7-5, 6-0
	1889	**W. Renshaw** v H.S. Barlow 3-6, 5-7, 8-6, 10-8, 8-6	**W. Renshaw** v E. Renshaw 6-4, 6-1, 3-6, 6-0
	1890	**W.J. Hamilton** v H.S. Barlow 2-6, 6-4, 6-4, 4-6, 7-5	**W.J. Hamilton** v W. Renshaw 6-8, 6-2, 3-6, 6-1, 6-1
	1891	**W. Baddeley** v J. Pim 6-4, 1-6, 7-5, 6-0	**W. Baddeley**: a bye W.J. Hamilton retired
	1892	**J. Pim** v E.W. Lewis 2-6, 5-7, 9-7, 6-3, 6-2	**W. Baddeley** v J. Pim 4-6, 6-3, 6-3, 6-2
	1893	**J. Pim** v H.S. Mahony 9-7, 6-3, 6-0	**J. Pim** v W. Baddeley 3-6, 6-1, 6-3, 6-2
	1894	**W. Baddeley** v E.W. Lewis 6-0, 6-1, 6-0	**J. Pim** v W. Baddeley 10-8, 6-2, 8-6
	1895	**W. Baddeley** v W.V. Eaves 4-6, 2-6, 8-6, 6-2, 6-3	**W. Baddeley**: a bye J. Pim retired
	1896	**H.S. Mahony** v W.V. Eaves 6-2, 6-2, 11-9	**H.S. Mahony** v W. Baddeley 6-2, 6-8, 5-7, 8-6, 6-3
	1897	**R.F. Doherty** v W.V. Eaves 6-3, 7-5, 2-0 retired	**R.F. Doherty** v H.S. Mahony 6-4, 6-4, 6-3
	1898	**H.L. Doherty** v H.S. Mahony 6-1, 6-2, 4-6, 2-6, 14-12	**R.F. Doherty** v H.L. Doherty 6-3, 6-3, 2-6, 5-7, 6-1
	1899	**A.W. Gore** v S.H. Smith 3-6, 6-2, 6-1, 6-4	**R.F. Doherty** v A.W. Gore 1-6, 4-6, 6-2, 6-3, 6-3
	1900	**S.H. Smith** v A.W. Gore 6-4, 4-6, 6-2, 6-1	**R.F. Doherty** v S.H. Smith 6-8, 6-3, 6-1, 6-2
	1901	**A.W. Gore** v C.P. Dixon 6-4, 6-0, 6-3	**A.W. Gore** v R.F. Doherty 4-6, 7-5, 6-4, 6-4
	1902	**H.L. Doherty** v M.J.G. Ritchie 8-6, 6-3, 7-5	**H.L. Doherty** v A.W. Gore 6-4, 6-3, 3-6, 6-0

Year	Final	Challenge Round
1903	**F.L. Riseley** v M.J.G. Ritchie 1-6, 6-3, 8-6, 13-11	**H.L. Doherty** v F.L. Riseley 7-5, 6-3, 6-0
1904	**F.L. Riseley** v M.J.G. Ritchie 6-0, 6-1, 6-2	**H.L. Doherty** v F.L. Riseley 6-1, 7-5, 8-6
1905	**N.E. Brookes** v S.H. Smith 1-6, 6-4, 6-1, 1-6, 7-5	**H.L. Doherty** v N.E. Brookes 8-6, 6-2, 6-4
1906	**F.L. Riseley** v A.W. Gore 6-3, 6-3, 6-4	**H.L. Doherty** v F.L. Riseley 6-4, 4-6, 6-2, 6-3
1907	**N.E. Brookes** v A.W. Gore 6-4, 6-4, 6-2	**N.E. Brookes**: a bye H. L. Doherty retired
1908	**A.W. Gore** v H. Roper Barrett 6-3, 6-2, 4-6, 3-6, 6-4	**A.W. Gore**: a bye N.E. Brookes retired
1909	**M.J.G. Ritchie** v H. Roper Barrett 6-2, 6-3, 4-6, 6-4	**A.W. Gore** v M.J.G. Ritchie 6-8, 1-6, 6-2, 6-2, 6-2
1910	**A.F. Wilding** v B.C. Wright 4-6, 4-6, 6-3, 6-2, 6-3	**A.F. Wilding** v A.W. Gore 6-4, 7-5, 4-6, 6-2
1911	**H. Roper Barrett** v C.P. Dixon 5-7, 4-6, 6-4, 6-3, 6-1	**A.F. Wilding** v H. Roper Barrett 6-4, 4-6, 2-6, 6-2, retired
1912	**A.W. Gore** v A.H. Gober 9-7, 2-6, 7-5, 6-1	**A.F. Wilding** v A.W. Gore 6-4, 6-4, 4-6, 6-4
1913	**M.E. McLoughlin** v S.N. Doust 6-3, 6-4, 7-5	**A.F. Wilding** v M.E. McLoughlin 8-6, 6-3, 10-8
1914	**N.E. Brookes** v O. Froitzheim 6-2, 6-1, 5-7, 4-6, 8-6	**N.E. Brookes** v A.F. Wilding 6-4, 6-4, 7-5
1915–18	No Competition	
1919	**G.L. Patterson** v A.R.F. Kingscote 6-2, 6-1, 6-3	**G.L. Patterson** v N.E. Brookes 6-3, 7-5, 6-2
1920	**W.T. Tilden** v Z. Shimizu 6-4, 6-4, 13-11	**W.T. Tilden** v G.L. Patterson 2-6, 6-3, 6-2, 6-4
1921	**B.I.C. Norton** v M. Alonso 5-7, 4-6, 7-5, 6-3, 6-3	**W.T. Tilden** v B.I.C. Norton 4-6, 2-6, 6-1, 6-0, 7-5

Year	Final	Year	Final
1922	**G.L. Patterson** v R. Lycett 6-3, 6-4, 6-2	1933	**J.H. Crawford** v H.E. Vines 4-6, 11-9, 6-2, 2-6, 6-4
1923	**W.M. Johnston** v F.T. Hunter 6-0, 6-3, 6-1	1934	**F.J. Perry** v J.H. Crawford 6-3, 6-0, 7-5
1924	**J. Borotra** v R. Lacoste 6-1, 3-6, 6-1, 3-6, 6-4	1935	**F.J. Perry** v G. von Cramm 6-2, 6-4, 6-4
1925	**R. Lacoste** v J. Borotra 6-3, 6-3, 4-6, 8-6	1936	**F.J. Perry** v G. von Cramm 6-1, 6-1, 6-0
1926	**J. Borotra** v H.O. Kinsey 8-6, 6-1, 6-3	1937	**J.D. Budge** v G. von Cramm 6-3, 6-4, 6-2
1927	**H. Cochet** v J. Borotra 4-6, 4-6, 6-3, 6-4, 7-5	1938	**J.D. Budge** v H.W. Austin 6-1, 6-0, 6-3
1928	**R. Lacoste** v H. Cochet 6-1, 4-6, 6-4, 6-2	1939	**R.L. Riggs** v E.T. Cooke 2-6, 8-6, 3-6, 6-3, 6-2
1929	**H. Cochet** v J. Borotra 6-4, 6-3, 6-4	1940–45	No Competition
1930	**W.T. Tilden** v W.L. Allison 6-3, 9-7, 6-4	1946	**Y. Petra** v G.E. Brown 6-2, 6-4, 7-9, 5-7, 6-4
1931	**S.B. Wood**: walk-over F.X. Shields scratched	1947	**J.A. Kramer** v T. Brown 6-1, 6-3, 6-2
1932	**H.E. Vines** v H.W. Austin 6-4, 6-2, 6-0	1948	**R. Falkenburg** v J.E. Bromwich 7-5, 0-6, 6-2, 3-6, 7-5

Year	Final	Year	Final
1949	**F.R. Schroeder** v J. Drobny 3-6, 6-0, 6-3, 4-6, 6-4	1964	**R.S. Emerson** v F.S. Stolle 6-4, 12-10, 4-6, 6-3
1950	**J.E. Patty** v F.A. Sedgman 6-1, 8-10, 6-2, 6-3	1965	**R.S. Emerson** v F.S. Stolle 6-2, 6-4, 6-4
1951	**R. Savitt** v K. McGregor 6-4, 6-4, 6-4	1966	**M. Santana** v R.D. Ralston 6-4, 11-9, 6-4
1952	**F.A. Sedgman** v J. Drobny 4-6, 6-2, 6-3, 6-2	1967	**J.D. Newcombe** v W.P. Bungert 6-3, 6-1, 6-1
1953	**E.V. Seixas** v K. Nielsen 9-7, 6-3, 6-4	1968	Open Championships began **R.G. Laver** v A.D. Roche 6-3, 6-4, 6-2
1954	**J. Drobny** v K.R. Rosewall 13-11, 4-6, 6-2, 9-7	1969	**R.G. Laver** v J.D. Newcombe 6-4, 5-7, 6-4, 6-4
1955	**M.A. Trabert** v K. Nielsen 6-3, 7-5, 6-1	1970	**J.D. Newcombe** v K.R. Rosewall 5-7, 6-3, 6-2, 3-6, 6-1
1956	**L.A. Hoad** v K.R. Rosewall 6-2, 4-6, 7-5, 6-4	1971	**J.D. Newcombe** v S.R. Smith 6-3, 5-7, 2-6, 6-4, 6-4
1957	**L.A. Hoad** v A.J. Cooper 6-2, 6-1, 6-2	1972	**S.R. Smith** v I. Nastase 4-6, 6-3, 6-3, 4-6, 7-5
1958	**A.J. Cooper** v N.A. Fraser 3-6, 6-3, 6-4, 13-11	1973	**J. Kodes** v A. Metreveli 6-1, 9-8, 6-3
1959	**A. Olmedo** v R.G. Laver 6-4, 6-3, 6-4	1974	**J.S. Connors** v K.R. Rosewall 6-1, 6-1, 6-4
1960	**N.A. Fraser** v R.G. Laver 6-4, 3-6, 9-7, 7-5	1975	**A.R. Ashe** v J.S. Connors 6-1, 6-1, 5-7, 6-4
1961	**R.G. Laver** v C.R. McKinley 6-3, 6-1, 6-4	1976	**B. Borg** v I. Nastase 6-4, 6-2, 9-7
1962	**R.G. Laver** v M.F. Mulligan 6-2, 6-2, 6-1		
1963	**C.R. McKinley** v F.S. Stolle 9-7, 6-1, 6-4		

Men's Doubles

Year	Final	Challenge Round
1879	**L.R. Erskine/H.F. Lawford** v F. Durant/G.E. Tabor	
1880	**W. Renshaw/E. Renshaw** v O.E. Woodhouse/C.J. Cole	
1881	**W. Renshaw/E. Renshaw** v W. J. Down/H. Vaughan	
1882	**J.T. Hartley/R.T. Richardson** v J.G. Horn/C.B. Russell	
1883	**C.W. Grinstead/C.E. Welldon** v C.B. Russell/R.T. Milford	
1884	**W. Renshaw/E. Renshaw** v E.W. Lewis/E.L. Williams 6-3, 3-6, 6-1, 1-6, 6-4	
1885	**W. Renshaw/E. Renshaw** v C.E. Farrar/A.J. Stanley 6-3, 6-3, 10-8	
1886	**C.E. Farrar/A.J. Stanley** v H.W.W. Wilberforce/P.B. Lyon 7-5, 6-3, 6-1	**W. Renshaw/E. Renshaw** v C.E. Farrar/A.J. Stanley 6-3, 6-3, 4-6, 7-5
1887	**H.W.W. Wilberforce/P.B. Lyon** v J.H. Crispe/E. Barratt Smith 7-5, 6-3, 6-2	**H.W.W. Wilberforce/P.B. Lyon**: a bye W. Renshaw/E. Renshaw retired

Year	Final	Challenge Round

Year	Final	Challenge Round
1909	**A.W. Gore/H. Roper Barrett** v S.N. Doust/H.A. Parker 6-2, 6-1, 6-4	**A.W. Gore/H. Roper Barrett**: a bye M.J.G. Ritchie/A.F. Wilding retired
1910	**A.F. Wilding/M.J.G. Ritchie** v K. Powell/R.B. Powell 9-7, 6-0, 6-4	**A.F. Wilding/M.J.G. Ritchie** v A.W. Gore/H. Roper Barrett 6-1, 6-1, 6-2
1911	**A.H. Gobert/M. Decugis** v J.C. Parke/S. Hardy 6-2, 6-1, 6-2	**A.H. Gobert/M. Decugis** v M.J.G. Ritchie/A.F. Wilding 9-7, 5-7, 6-3, 2-6, 6-2
1912	**H. Roper Barrett/ C.P. Dixon** v J.C. Parke/A.E. Beamish 6-8, 6-4, 3-6, 6-3, 6-4	**H. Roper Barrett/C.P. Dixon** v A.H. Gobert/M. Decugis 3-6, 6-3, 6-4, 7-5
1913	**F.W. Rahe/H. Kleinschroth** v J.C. Parke/A.E. Beamish 6-3, 6-2, 6-4	**H. Roper Barrett/C.P. Dixon** v F.W. Rahe/H. Kleinschroth 6-2, 6-4, 4-6, 6-2
1914	**N.E. Brookes/A.F. Wilding** v F.G. Lowe/A.H. Lowe 6-2, 8-6, 6-1	**N.E. Brookes/A.F. Wilding** v H. Roper Barrett/C.P. Dixon 6-1, 6-1, 5-7, 8-6
1915–18	No Competition	
1919	**R.V. Thomas/P. O'Hara Wood** v R. Lycett/R.W. Heath 6-4, 6-2, 4-6, 6-2	Walk over
1920	**R.N. Williams/C.S. Garland** v A.R.F. Kingscote/J.C. Parke 4-6, 6-4, 7-5, 6-2	**R.N. Williams/C.S. Garland**: a bye R.V. Thomas/P. O'Hara Wood retired
1921	**R. Lycett/M. Woosnam** v F.G. Lowe/A.H. Lowe 6-3, 6-0, 7-5	**R. Lycett/M. Woosnam**: a bye R.N. Williams/C.S. Garland retired

Year	Final	Year	Final
1922	**J.O. Anderson/R. Lycett** v G.L. Patterson/P. O'Hara Wood 3-6, 7-9, 6-4, 6-3, 11-9	1933	**J. Borotra/J. Brugnon** v R. Nunoi/J. Sato 4-6, 6-3, 6-3, 7-5
1923	**R. Lycett/L.A. Godfree** v Count de Gomar/E. Flaquer 6-3, 6-4, 3-6, 6-3	1934	**G.M. Lott/L.R. Stoefen** v J. Borotra/J. Brugnon 6-2, 6-3, 6-4
1924	**V. Richards/F.T. Hunter** v R.N. Williams/W.M. Washburn 6-3, 3-6, 8-10, 8-6, 6-3	1935	**J.H. Crawford/A.K. Quist** v W.L. Allison/J. Van Ryn 6-3, 5-7, 6-2, 5-7, 7-5
1925	**R. Lacoste/J. Borotra** v J. Hennessey/R. Casey 6-4, 11-9, 4-6, 1-6, 6-3	1936	**G.P. Hughes/C.R.D. Tuckey** v C.E. Hare/F.H.D. Wilde 6-4, 3-6, 7-9, 6-1, 6-4
1926	**H. Cochet/J. Brugnon** v V. Richards/H.O. Kinsey 7-5, 4-6, 6-3, 6-2	1937	**J.D. Budge/C.G. Mako** v G.P. Hughes/C.R.D. Tuckey 6-0, 6-4, 6-8, 6-1
1927	**F.T. Hunter/W.T. Tilden** v J. Brugnon/H. Cochet 1-6, 4-6, 8-6, 6-3, 6-4	1938	**J.D. Budge/C.G. Mako** v H. Henkel/G. von Metaxa 6-4, 3-6, 6-3, 8-6
1928	**H. Cochet/J. Brugnon** v G.L. Patterson/J.B. Hawkes 13-11, 6-4, 6-4	1939	**E.T. Cooke/R.L. Riggs** v C.E. Hare/F.H.D. Wilde 6-3, 3-6, 6-3, 9-7
1929	**W.L. Allison/J. Van Ryn** v J.C. Gregory/I.G. Collins 6-4, 5-7, 6-3, 10-12, 6-4	1940–45	No Competition
1930	**W.L. Allison/J. Van Ryn** v J.H. Doeg/G.M. Lott 6-3, 6-3, 6-2	1946	**T. Brown/J.A. Kramer** G.E. Brown/D. Pails 6-4, 6-4, 6-2
1931	**G.M. Lott/J. Van Ryn** v H. Cochet/J. Brugnon 6-2, 10-8, 9-11, 3-6, 6-3	1947	**R. Falkenburg/J.A. Kramer** v A.J. Mottram/O.W. Sidwell 8-6, 6-3, 6-3
1932	**J. Borotra/J. Brugnon** v G.P. Hughes/F.J. Perry 6-0, 4-6, 3-6, 7-5, 7-5	1948	**J.E. Bromwich/F.A. Sedgman** v T. Brown/G. Mulloy 5-7, 7-5, 7-5, 9-7

Year	Final	Year	Final
1949	**R.P. Gonzalez/F.A. Parker** v G. Mulloy/F.R. Schroeder 6-4, 6-4, 6-2	1963	**R.H. Osuna/A. Palafox** v J.C. Barclay/P. Darmon 4-6, 6-2, 6-2, 6-2
1950	**J.E. Bromwich/A.K. Quist** v G.E. Brown/O.W. Sidwell 7-5, 3-6, 6-3, 3-6, 6-2	1964	**R.A.J. Hewitt/F.S. Stolle** v R. Emerson/K.N. Fletcher 7-5, 11-9, 6-4
1951	**K. McGregor/F.A. Sedgman** v J. Drobný/E.W. Sturgess 3-6, 6-2, 6-3, 3-6, 6-3	1965	**J.D. Newcombe/A.D. Roche** v K.N. Fletcher/R.A.J. Hewitt 7-5, 6-3, 6-4
1952	**K. McGregor/F.A. Sedgman** v E.V. Seixas/E.W. Sturgess 6-3, 7-5, 6-4	1966	**K.N. Fletcher/J.D. Newcombe** v W.W. Bowrey/O.K. Davidson 6-3, 6-4, 3-6, 6-3
1953	**L.A. Hoad/K.R. Rosewall** v R.N. Hartwig/M.G. Rose 6-4, 7-5, 4-6, 7-5	1967	**R.A.J. Hewitt/F.D. McMillan** v R. Emerson/K.N. Fletcher 6-2, 6-3, 6-4
1954	**R.N. Hartwig/M.G. Rose** v E.V. Seixas/M.A. Trabert 6-4, 6-4, 3-6, 6-4	1968	Open Championships began **J.D. Newcombe/A.D. Roche** v K.R. Rosewall/F.S. Stolle 3-6, 8-6, 5-7, 14-12, 6-3
1955	**R.N. Hartwig/L.A. Hoad** v N.A. Fraser/K.R. Rosewall 7-5, 6-4, 6-3	1969	**J.D. Newcombe/A.D. Roche** v T.S. Okker/M.C. Riessen 7-5, 11-9, 6-3
1956	**L.A. Hoad/K.R. Rosewall** v N. Pietrangeli/O. Sirola 7-5, 6-2, 6-1	1970	**J.D. Newcombe/A.D. Roche** v K.R. Rosewall/F.S. Stolle 10-8, 6-3, 6-1
1957	**G. Mulloy/J.E. Patty** v N.A. Fraser/L.A. Hoad 8-10, 6-4, 6-4, 6-4	1971	**R.S. Emerson/R.G. Laver** v A.R. Ashe/R.D. Ralston 4-6, 9-7, 6-8, 6-4, 6-4
1958	**S. Davidson/U. Schmidt** v A.J. Cooper/N.A. Fraser 6-4, 6-4, 8-6	1972	**R.A.J. Hewitt/F.D. McMillan** v S.R. Smith/E.J. Van Dillen 6-2, 6-2, 9-7
1959	**R. Emerson/N.A. Fraser** v R.G. Laver/R. Mark 8-6, 6-3, 14-16, 9-7	1973	**J.S. Connors/I. Nastase** v J.R. Cooper/N.A. Fraser 3-6, 6-3, 6-4, 8-9, 6-1
1960	**R.H. Osuna/R.D. Ralston** v M.G. Davis/R.K. Wilson 7-5, 6-3, 10-8	1974	**J.D. Newcombe/A.D. Roche** v R.C. Lutz/S.R. Smith 8-6, 6-4, 6-4
1961	**R. Emerson/N.A. Fraser** v R.A.J. Hewitt/F.S. Stolle 6-4, 6-8, 6-4, 6-8, 8-6	1975	**V. Gerulaitis/A. Mayer** v C. Dowdeswell/A.J. Stone 7-5, 8-6, 6-4
1962	**R.A.J. Hewitt/F.S. Stolle** v B. Jovanović/N. Pilić 6-2, 5-7, 6-2, 6-4	1976	**B. Gottfried/R. Ramirez** v R.L. Case/G. Masters 3-6, 6-3, 8-6, 2-6, 7-5

Women's Singles

Year	Final	Challenge Round
1884	**Miss M.Watson** v Miss L. Watson 6-8, 6-3, 6-3	
1885	**Miss M. Watson** v Miss B. Bingley 6-1, 7-5	
1886	**Miss B. Bingley** v Miss A. Tabor 6-2, 6-1	**Miss B. Bingley** v Miss M. Watson 6-3, 6-3
1887	**Miss L. Dod** v Mrs C.J. Cole 6-2, 6-3	**Miss L. Dod** v Miss B. Bingley 6-2, 6-0
1888	**Mrs G.W. Hillyard** v Miss Howes 6-1, 6-2	**Miss L. Dod** v Mrs G.W. Hillyard 6-3, 6-3
1889	**Mrs G.W. Hillyard** v Miss L. Rice 4-6, 8-6, 6-4	**Mrs G.W. Hillyard**: a bye Miss L. Dod retired
1890	**Miss L. Rice** v Miss Jacks 6-4, 6-1	**Miss L. Rice**: a bye Mrs G.W. Hillyard retired
1891	**Miss L. Dod** v Mrs G.W. Hillyard 6-2, 6-1	**Miss L. Dod**: a bye Miss L. Rice retired

Year	Final	Challenge Round
1892	**Mrs G.W. Hillyard** v Miss M. Shackle 6-1, 6-4	**Miss L. Dod** v Mrs G.W. Hillyard 6-1, 6-1
1893	**Mrs G.W. Hillyard** v Miss M. Shackle 6-3, 6-2	**Miss L. Dod** v Mrs G.W. Hillyard 6-8, 6-1, 6-4
1894	**Mrs G.W. Hillyard** v Miss L. Austin 6-1, 6-1	**Mrs G.W. Hillyard**: a bye Miss L. Dod retired
1895	**Miss C. Cooper** v Miss Jackson 7-5, 8-6	**Miss C. Cooper**: a bye Mrs G.W. Hillyard retired
1896	**Mrs Pickering** v Miss L. Austin 4-6, 6-3, 6-3	**Miss C. Cooper** v Mrs Pickering 6-2, 6-3
1897	**Mrs G.W. Hillyard** v Mrs Pickering 6-2, 7-5	**Mrs G.W. Hillyard** v Miss C. Cooper 5-7, 7-5, 6-2
1898	**Miss C. Cooper** v Miss Martin 6-4, 6-4	**Miss C. Cooper**: a bye Mrs G.W. Hillyard retired
1899	**Mrs G.W. Hillyard** v Mrs R. Durlacher 7-5, 6-8, 6-1	**Mrs G.W. Hillyard** v Miss C. Cooper 6-2, 6-3
1900	**Miss C. Cooper** v Miss Martin 8-6, 5-7, 6-1	**Mrs G.W. Hillyard** v Miss C. Cooper 4-6, 6-4, 6-4
1901	**Mrs A. Sterry** v Miss Martin 6-3, 6-4	**Mrs A. Sterry** v Mrs G.W. Hillyard 6-2, 6-2
1902	**Miss M.E. Robb** v Miss A.M. Morton 6-2, 6-4	**Miss M.E. Robb** v Mrs A. Sterry 7-5, 6-1
1903	**Miss D.K. Douglass** v Miss E.W. Thomson 4-6, 6-4, 6-2	**Miss D.K. Douglass**: a bye Miss M.E. Robb retired
1904	**Mrs A. Sterry** v Miss A.M. Morton 6-3, 6-3	**Miss D.K. Douglass** v Mrs A. Sterry 6-0, 6-3
1905	**Miss M.G. Sutton** v Miss C.M. Wilson 6-3, 8-6	**Miss M.G. Sutton** v Miss D.K. Douglass 6-3, 6-4
1906	**Miss D.K. Douglass** v Mrs A. Sterry 6-2, 6-2	**Miss D.K. Douglass** v Miss M.G. Sutton 6-3, 9-7
1907	**Miss M.G. Sutton** v Miss C.M. Wilson 6-4, 6-2	**Miss M.G. Sutton** v Mrs Lambert Chambers 6-1, 6-4
1908	**Mrs A. Sterry** v Miss A.M. Morton 6-4, 6-4	**Mrs A. Sterry**: a bye Miss M.G. Sutton retired
1909	**Miss D.P. Boothby** v Miss A.M. Morton 6-4, 4-6, 8-6	**Miss D.P. Boothby**: a bye Mrs A. Sterry retired
1910	**Mrs Lambert Chambers** v Miss E.G. Johnson 6-4, 6-2	**Mrs Lambert Chambers** v Miss D.P. Boothby 6-2, 6-2
1911	**Miss D.P. Boothby** v Mrs Hannam 6-2, 7-5	**Mrs Lambert Chambers** v Miss D.P. Boothby 6-0, 6-0
1912	**Mrs D.R. Larcombe** v Mrs A. Sterry 6-3, 6-1	**Mrs D.R. Larcombe**: a bye Mrs Lambert Chambers retired
1913	**Mrs Lambert Chambers** v Mrs R.J. McNair 6-0, 6-4	**Mrs Lambert Chambers**: a bye Mrs D.R. Larcombe retired
1914	**Mrs D.R. Larcombe** v Miss E. Ryan 6-3, 6-2	**Mrs Lambert Chambers** v Mrs D.R. Larcombe 7-5, 6-4
1915–18	No Competition	
1919	**Miss S. Lenglen** v Mrs P. Satterthwaite 6-1, 6-1	**Miss S. Lenglen** v Mrs Lambert Chambers 10-8, 4-6, 9-7

Year	Final		Challenge Round
1920	**Mrs Lambert Chambers** v Miss E. Ryan 6-2, 6-1		**Miss S. Lenglen** v Mrs Lambert Chambers 6-3, 6-0
1921	**Miss E. Ryan** v Mrs P. Satterthwaite 6-1, 6-0		**Miss S. Lenglen** v Miss E. Ryan 6-2, 6-0

Year	Final	Year	Final
1922	**Miss S. Lenglen** v Mrs M. Mallory 6-2, 6-0	1952	**Miss M. Connolly** v Miss A.L. Brough 7-5, 6-3
1923	**Miss S. Lenglen** v Miss K. McKane 6-2, 6-2	1953	**Miss M. Connolly** v Miss D.J. Hart 8-6, 7-5
1924	**Miss K. McKane** v Miss H. Wills 4-6, 6-4, 6-4	1954	**Miss M. Connolly** v Miss A.L. Brough 6-2, 7-5
1925	**Miss S. Lenglen** v Miss J. Fry 6-2, 6-0	1955	**Miss A.L. Brough** v Mrs J.G. Fleitz 7-5, 8-6
1926	**Mrs L.A. Godfree** v Miss L. de Alvarez 6-2, 4-6, 6-3	1956	**Miss S.J. Fry** v Miss A. Buxton 6-3, 6-1
1927	**Miss H. Wills** v Miss L. de Alvarez 6-2, 6-4	1957	**Miss A. Gibson** v Miss D.R. Hard 6-3, 6-2
1928	**Miss H. Wills** v Miss L. de Alvarez 6-2, 6-3	1958	**Miss A. Gibson** v Miss A. Mortimer 8-6, 6-2
1929	**Miss H. Wills** v Miss H.H. Jacobs 6-1, 6-2	1959	**Miss M.E. Bueno** v Miss D.R. Hard 6-4, 6-3
1930	**Mrs F.S. Moody** v Miss E. Ryan 6-2, 6-2	1960	**Miss M.E. Bueno** v Miss S. Reynolds 8-6, 6-0
1931	**Miss C. Aussem** v Miss H. Krahwinkel 6-2, 7-5	1961	**Miss A. Mortimer** v Miss C.C. Truman 4-6, 6-4, 7-5
1932	**Mrs F.S. Moody** v Miss H.H. Jacobs 6-3, 6-1	1962	**Mrs J.R. Susman** v Mrs V. Suková 6-4, 6-4
1933	**Mrs F.S. Moody** v Miss D.E. Round 6-4, 6-8, 6-3	1963	**Miss M. Smith** v Miss B.J. Moffitt 6-3, 6-4
1934	**Miss D.E. Round** v Miss H.H. Jacobs 6-2, 5-7, 6-3	1964	**Miss M.E. Bueno** v Miss M. Smith 6-4, 7-9, 6-3
1935	**Mrs F.S. Moody** v Miss H.H. Jacobs 6-3, 3-6, 7-5	1965	**Miss M. Smith** v Miss M.E. Bueno 6-4, 7-5
1936	**Miss H.H. Jacobs** v Mrs S. Sperling 6-2, 4-6, 7-5	1966	**Mrs L.W. King** v Miss M.E. Bueno 6-3, 3-6, 6-1
1937	**Miss D.E. Round** v Miss J. Jedrzejowska 6-2, 2-6, 7-5	1967	**Mrs L.W. King** v Mrs P.F. Jones 6-3, 6-4
1938	**Mrs F.S. Moody** v Miss H.H. Jacobs 6-4, 6-0	1968	Open Championships began **Mrs L.W. King** v Miss J.A.M. Tegart 9-7, 7-5
1939	**Miss A. Marble** v Miss K.E. Stammers 6-2, 6-0	1969	**Mrs P.F. Jones** v Mrs L.W. King 3-6, 6-3, 6-2
1940–45	No Competition	1970	**Mrs B.M. Court** v Mrs L.W. King 14-12, 11-9
1946	**Miss P.M. Betz** v Miss A.L. Brough 6-2, 6-4	1971	**Miss E.F. Goolagong** v Mrs B.M. Court 6-4, 6-1
1947	**Miss M.E. Osborne** v Miss D.J. Hart 6-2, 6-4	1972	**Mrs L.W. King** v Miss E.F. Goolagong 6-3, 6-3
1948	**Miss A.L. Brough** v Miss D.J. Hart 6-3, 8-6	1973	**Mrs L.W. King** v Miss C. Evert 6-0, 7-5
1949	**Miss A.L. Brough** v Mrs. W. duPont 10-8, 1-6, 10-8	1974	**Miss C.M. Evert** v Mrs O. Morozova 6-0, 6-4
1950	**Miss A.L. Brough** v Mrs W. duPont 6-1, 3-6, 6-1	1975	**Mrs L.W. King** v Mrs R. Cawley 6-0, 6-1
1951	**Miss D.J. Hart** v Miss S.J. Fry 6-1, 6-0	1976	**Miss C.M. Evert** v Mrs R. Cawley 6-3, 4-6, 8-6

Women's Doubles

Year	Final	Year	Final
1913	**Mrs R.J. McNair/Miss D.P. Boothby** v Mrs A. Sterry/Mrs Lambert Chambers 4-6, 2-4 retired	1936	**Miss F. James/Miss K.E. Stammers** v Mrs S.P. Fabyan/Miss H.H. Jacobs 6-2, 6-1
1914	**Miss E. Ryan/Miss A.M. Morton** v Mrs D. R.. Larcombe/Mrs Hannam 6-1, 6-3	1937	**Mrs R. Mathieu/Miss A.M. Yorke** v Mrs M.R. King/Mrs J.B. Pittman 6-3, 6-3
1915–18	No Competition	1938	**Mrs S.P. Fabyan/Miss A. Marble** v Mrs R. Mathieu/Miss A.M. Yorke 6-2, 6-3
1919	**Miss S. Lenglen/Miss E. Ryan** v Mrs Lambert Chambers/Mrs D.R. Larcombe 4-6, 7-5, 6-3	1939	**Mrs S.P. Fabyan/Miss A. Marble** v Miss H.H. Jacobs/Miss A.M. Yorke 6-1, 6-0
1920	**Miss S. Lenglen/Miss E. Ryan** v Mrs Lambert Chambers/Mrs D.R. Larcombe 6-4, 6-0	1940–45	No Competition
1921	**Miss S. Lenglen/Miss E. Ryan** v Mrs A.E. Beamish/Mrs I.E. Peacock 6-1, 6-2	1946	**Miss A.L. Brough/Miss M.E. Osborne** v Miss P.M. Betz/Miss D.J. Hart 6-3, 2-6, 6-3
1922	**Miss S. Lenglen/Miss E. Ryan** v Mrs A.D. Stocks/Miss K. McKane 6-0, 6-4	1947	**Miss D.J. Hart/Mrs P.C. Todd** v Miss A.L. Brough/Miss M.E. Osborne 3-6, 6-4, 7-5
1923	**Miss S. Lenglen/Miss E. Ryan** v Miss J. Austin/Miss E.L. Colyer 6-3, 6-1	1948	**Miss A.L. Brough/Mrs W. duPont** v Miss D.J. Hart/Mrs P.C. Todd 6-3, 3-6, 6-3
1924	**Mrs G.W. Wightman/Miss H. Wills** v Mrs B.C. Covell/Miss K. McKane 6-4, 6-4	1949	**Miss A.L. Brough/Mrs W. duPont** v Miss G. Moran/Mrs P.C. Todd 8-6, 7-5
1925	**Miss S. Lenglen/Miss E. Ryan** v Mrs A.V. Bridge/Mrs C.G. McIlquham 6-2, 6-2	1950	**Miss A.L. Brough/Mrs W. duPont** v Miss S.J. Fry/Miss D.J. Hart 6-4, 5-7, 6-1
1926	**Miss E. Ryan/Miss M.K. Browne** v Mrs L.A. Godfree/Miss E.L. Colyer 6-1, 6-1	1951	**Miss S.J. Fry/Miss D.J. Hart** v Miss A.L. Brough/Mrs W. duPont 6-3, 13-11
1927	**Miss H. Wills/Miss E. Ryan** v Miss F.L. Heine/Mrs I.E. Peacock 6-3, 6-2	1952	**Miss S.J. Fry/Miss D.J. Hart** v Miss A.L. Brough/Miss M. Connolly 8-6, 6-3
1928	**Mrs Holcroft-Watson/Miss P. Saunders** v Miss E.H. Harvey/Miss E.B. Bennett 6-2, 6-3	1953	**Miss S.J. Fry/Miss D.J. Hart** v Miss M. Connolly/Miss J. Sampson 6-0, 6-0
1929	**Mrs Holcroft-Watson/Mrs L.R.C. Michell** v Mrs B.C. Covell/Mrs D.C. Shepherd-Barron 6-4, 8-6	1954	**Miss A.L. Brough/Mrs W. duPont** v Miss S.J. Fry/Miss D.J. Hart 4-6, 9-7, 6-3
1930	**Mrs F.S. Moody/Miss E. Ryan** v Miss E. Cross/Miss S. Palfrey 6-2, 9-7	1955	**Miss A. Mortimer/Miss J.A. Shilcock** v Miss S.J. Bloomer/Miss P.E. Ward 7-5, 6-1
1931	**Mrs D.C. Shepherd-Barron/Miss P.E. Mudford** v Miss D. Metaxa/Miss J. Sigart 3-6, 6-3, 6-4	1956	**Miss A. Buxton/Miss A. Gibson** v Miss F. Muller/Miss D.G. Seeney 6-1, 8-6
1932	**Miss D. Metaxa/Miss J. Sigart** v Miss E. Ryan/Miss H.H. Jacobs 6-4, 6-3	1957	**Miss A. Gibson/Miss D.R. Hard** v Mrs K. Hawton/Mrs T.D. Long 6-1, 6-2
1933	**Mrs R. Mathieu/Miss E. Ryan** v Miss F. James/Miss A.M. Yorke 6-2, 9-11, 6-4	1958	**Miss M.E. Bueno/Miss A. Gibson** v Mrs W. duPont/Miss M. Varner 6-3, 7-5
1934	**Mrs R. Mathieu/Miss E. Ryan** v Mrs D. Andrus/Mrs S. Henrotin 6-3, 6-3	1959	**Miss J. Arth/Miss D.R. Hard** v Mrs J.G. Fleitz/Miss C.C. Truman 2-6, 6-2, 6-3
1935	**Miss F. James/Miss K.E. Stammers** v Mrs R. Mathieu/Mrs S. Sperling 6-1, 6-4	1960	**Miss M.E. Bueno/Miss D.R. Hard** v Miss S. Reynolds/Miss R. Schuurman 6-4, 6-0

Year	Final	Year	Final
1961	**Miss K. Hantze/Miss B.J. Moffitt** v Miss J. Lehane/Miss M. Smith 6-3, 6-4	1969	**Mrs B.M. Court/Miss J.A.M. Tegart** v Miss P.S.A. Hogan/Miss M. Michel 9-7, 6-2
1962	**Miss B.J. Moffitt/Mrs J.R. Susman** v Mrs L.E.G. Price/Miss R. Schuurman 5-7, 6-3, 7-5	1970	**Miss R. Casals/Mrs L.W. King** v Miss F. Durr/Miss S.V. Wade 6-2, 6-3
1963	**Miss M.E. Bueno/Miss D.R. Hard** v Miss R.A. Ebbern/Miss M. Smith 8-6, 9-7	1971	**Miss R. Casals/Mrs L.W. King** v Mrs. B.M. Court/Miss E.F. Goolagong 6-3, 6-2
1964	**Miss M. Smith/Miss L.R. Turner** v Miss B.J. Moffitt/Mrs J.R. Susman 7-5, 6-2	1972	**Mrs L.W. King/Miss B.F. Stöve** v Mrs D.E. Dalton/Miss F. Durr 6-2, 4-6, 6-3
1965	**Miss M.E. Bueno/Miss B.J. Moffitt** v Miss F. Durr/Miss J. Lieffrig 6-2, 7-5	1973	**Miss R. Casals/Mrs L.W. King** v Miss F. Durr/Miss B.F. Stöve 6-1, 4-6, 7-5
1966	**Miss M.E. Bueno/Miss N. Richey** v Miss M. Smith/Miss J.A.M. Tegart 6-3, 4-6, 6-4	1974	**Miss E.F. Goolagong/Miss M. Michel** v Miss H.F. Gourlay/Miss K.M. Krantzcke 2-6, 6-4, 6-3
1967	**Miss R. Casals/Mrs L.W. King** v Miss M.E. Bueno/Miss N. Richey 9-11, 6-4, 6-2	1975	**Miss A.K. Kiyomura/Miss K. Sawamatsu** v Miss F. Durr/Miss B.F. Stöve 7-5, 1-6, 7-5
1968	Open Championships began **Miss R. Casals/Mrs L.W. King** v Miss F. Durr/Mrs P.F. Jones 3-6, 6-4, 7-5	1976	**Miss C. Evert/Miss M. Navratilova** v Mrs L.W. King/Miss B.F. Stöve 6-1, 3-6, 7-5

Mixed Doubles

Year	Final	Year	Final
1913	**H. Crisp/Mrs C.O. Tuckey** v J.C. Parke/Mrs D.R. Larcombe 3-6, 5-3 retired	1928	**P.D.B. Spence/Miss E. Ryan** v J.H. Crawford/Miss D. Akhurst 7-5, 6-4
1914	**J.C. Parke/Mrs D.R. Larcombe** v A.F. Wilding/Miss M. Broquedis 4-6, 6-4, 6-2	1929	**F.T. Hunter/Miss H. Wills** v I.G. Collins/Miss J. Fry 6-1, 6-4
1915–18	No Competition	1930	**J.H. Crawford/Miss E. Ryan** v D. Prenn/Miss H. Krahwinkel 6-1, 6-3
1919	**R. Lycett/Miss E. Ryan** v A.D. Prebble/Mrs Lambert Chambers 6-0, 6-0	1931	**G.M. Lott/Mrs L.A. Harper** v I.G. Collins/Miss J.C. Ridley 6-3, 1-6, 6-1
1920	**G.L. Patterson/Miss S. Lenglen** v R. Lycett/Miss E. Ryan 7-5, 6-3	1932	**F. Maier/Miss E. Ryan** v H.C. Hopman/Miss J. Sigart 7-5, 6-2
1921	**R. Lycett/Miss E. Ryan** v M. Woosnam/Miss P.L. Howkins 6-3, 6-1	1933	**G. von Cramm/Miss H. Krahwinkel** v N.G. Farquharson/Miss M. Heeley 7-5, 8-6
1922	**P. O'Hara Wood/Miss S. Lenglen** v R. Lycett/Miss E. Ryan 6-4, 6-3	1934	**R. Miki/Miss D.E. Round** v H.W. Austin/Mrs D.C. Shepherd-Barron 3-6, 6-4, 6-0
1923	**R. Lycett/Miss E. Ryan** v L.S. Deane/Mrs D.C. Shepherd-Barron 6-4, 7-5	1935	**F.J. Perry/Miss D.E. Round** v H.C. Hopman/Mrs H.C. Hopman 7-5, 4-6, 6-2
1924	**J.B. Gilbert/Miss K. McKane** v L.A. Godfree/Mrs D.C. Shepherd-Barron 6-3, 3-6, 6-3	1936	**F.J. Perry/Miss D.E. Round** v J.D. Budge/Mrs S.P. Fabyan 7-9, 7-5, 6-4
1925	**J. Borotra/Miss S. Lenglen** v H.L. de Morpurgo/Miss E. Ryan 6-3, 6-3	1937	**J.D. Budge/Miss A. Marble** v Y. Petra/Mrs R. Mathieu 6-4, 6-1
1926	**L.A. Godfree/Mrs L.A. Godfree** v H.O. Kinsey/Miss M.K. Browne 6-3, 6-4	1938	**J.D. Budge/Miss A. Marble** v H. Henkel/Mrs S.P. Fabyan 6-1, 6-4
1927	**F.T. Hunter/Miss E. Ryan** v L.A. Godfree/Mrs L.A. Godfree 8-6, 6-0	1939	**R.L. Riggs/Miss A. Marble** v F.H.D. Wilde/Miss N.B. Brown 9-7, 6-1

Year	Final	Year	Final
1940–45	No Competition		
1946	**T. Brown/Miss A.L. Brough** v G.E. Brown/Miss D. Bundy 6-4, 6-4	1962	**N.A. Fraser/Mrs W. duPont** v R.D. Ralston/Miss A.S. Haydon 2-6, 6-3, 13-11
1947	**J.E. Bromwich/Miss A.L. Brough** v C.F. Long/Mrs N.M. Bolton 1-6, 6-4, 6-2	1963	**K.N. Fletcher/Miss M. Smith** v R.A.J. Hewitt/Miss D.R. Hard 11-9, 6-4
1948	**J.E. Bromwich/Miss A.L. Brough** v F.A. Sedgman/Miss D.J. Hart 6-2, 3-6, 6-3	1964	**F.S. Stolle/Miss L.R. Turner** v K.N. Fletcher/Miss M. Smith 6-4, 6-4
1949	**E.W. Sturgess/Mrs S.P. Summers** v J.E. Bromwich/Miss A.L. Brough 9-7, 9-11, 7-5	1965	**K.N. Fletcher/Miss M. Smith** v A.D. Roche/Miss J.A.M. Tegart 12-10, 6-3
1950	**E.W. Sturgess/Miss A.L. Brough** v G.E. Brown/Mrs P.C. Todd 11-9, 1-6, 6-4	1966	**K.N. Fletcher/Miss M. Smith** v R.D. Ralston/Mrs L.W. King 4-6, 6-3, 6-3
1951	**F.A. Sedgman/Miss D.J. Hart** v M.G. Rose/Mrs N.M. Bolton 7-5, 6-2	1967	**O.K. Davidson/Mrs L.W. King** v K.N. Fletcher/Miss M.E. Bueno 7-5, 6-2
1952	**F.A. Sedgman/Miss D.J. Hart** v E. Morea/Mrs T.D. Long 4-6, 6-3, 6-4	1968	Open Championships began **K.N. Fletcher/Mrs B.M. Court** v A. Metreveli/Miss O. Morozova 6-1, 14-12
1953	**E.V. Seixas/Miss D.J. Hart** v E. Morea/Miss S.J. Fry 9-7, 7-5	1969	**F.S. Stolle/Mrs P.F. Jones** v A.D. Roche/Miss J.A.M. Tegart 6-2, 6-3
1954	**E.V. Seixas/Miss D.J. Hart** v K.R Rosewall/Mrs W. duPont 5-7, 6-4, 6-3	1970	**I. Nastase/Miss R. Casals** v A. Metreveli/Miss O. Morozova 6-3, 4-6, 9-7
1955	**E.V. Seixas/Miss D.J. Hart** v E. Morea/Miss A.L. Brough 8-6, 2-6, 6-3	1971	**O.K. Davidson/Mrs L.W. King** v M.C. Riessen/Mrs B.M. Court 3-6, 6-2, 15-13
1956	**E.V. Seixas/Miss S.J. Fry** v G. Mulloy/Miss A. Gibson 2-6, 6-2, 7-5	1972	**I Nastase/Miss R. Casals** v K.G. Warwick/Miss E.F. Goolagong 6-4, 6-4
1957	**M.G. Rose/Miss D.R. Hard** v N.A. Fraser/Miss A. Gibson 6-4, 7-5	1973	**O.K. Davidson/Mrs L.W. King** v R. Ramirez/Miss J.S. Newberry 6-3, 6-2
1958	**R.N. Howe/Miss L. Coghlan** v K. Nielsen/Miss A. Gibson 6-3, 13-11	1974	**O.K. Davidson/Mrs L.W. King** v M.J. Farrell/Miss L.J. Charles 6-3, 9-7
1959	**R.G. Laver/Miss D.R. Hard** v N.A. Fraser/Miss M.E. Bueno 6-4, 6-3	1975	**M.C. Riessen/Mrs B.M. Court** v A.J. Stone/Miss Stöve 6-4, 7-5
1960	**R.G. Laver/Miss D.R. Hard** v R.N. Howe/Miss M.E. Bueno 13-11, 3-6, 8-6	1976	**A.D. Roche/Miss F. Durr** v R.L. Stockton/Miss R. Casals 6-3, 2-6, 7-5
1961	**F.S. Stolle/Miss L.R. Turner** v R.N. Howe/Miss E. Buding 11-9, 6-2		

Longest Matches

Men's Singles

Pancho Gonzales beat Charlie Pasarell: 22-24, 1-6, 16-14, 6-3, 11-9, in the first round, 1969.
Total games: 112

Men's Doubles

Budge Patty and Tony Trabert beat Frank Sedgman and Ken McGregor: 6-4, 31-29, 7-9, 6-2, in the quarter-finals, 1950.
Total games: 94

Women's Singles

Alice Weiwers beat Rita Anderson: 8-10, 14-12, 6-4, in the second round, 1948.
Total games: 54

Women's Doubles

Pat Brazier and Christabel Wheatcroft beat Mildred Nonweiler and Betty Soames: 11-9, 5-7, 9-7, in the first round, 1932.
Total games: 48

Mixed Doubles

Maria Bueno and Ken Fletcher beat Anna Dmitrieva and Alex Metreveli: 6-8, 7-5, 16-14, in the quarter-finals, 1967.
Total games: 56

Acknowledgments

Associated Press **52** top; Camera Press **10** left, **11** top left and bottom left, **13** top and bottom, **14** top and bottom, **43** bottom right, **57** right, **73** right, **75**; Central Press **8**, **10** right, **15** top, **18** bottom right, **22** top left, **25**, **27** bottom, **28** top and bottom, **31** left and right, **32** top left and bottom, **33** bottom right, **35** centre, **37** bottom right, **39** top left, **42** top centre, top right and bottom left, **52** bottom, **58** bottom, **60** top left and top right, **61** bottom, **65** right, **68** bottom right, **69** top, bottom left and bottom right, **70** top and bottom, **71** top and bottom, **76** right, **77** top left and bottom right, **81** left and bottom right; Illustrated London News **16**, **24** top, **27** top, **50** right, **51** bottom, **59** left; Keystone Press Agency **34** top right and bottom right, **35**, **36** top and bottom, **37** top, **38**, **39** top right and bottom, **41** top left, **43** top left, bottom left and top right, **44** left and right, **45** top, bottom left and bottom right, **46** bottom, **49**, **54** bottom, **55** top left, **63** right, **66** bottom, **73** left, **78** left, **79** top and bottom, **81** top right, back endpapers; Le-Roye Productions **17** top left and top right, **23**, **29** bottom right, **30** bottom right, **46** top, **57** left, **58** top left, **67** top and bottom, **68** bottom left, **74** top and bottom; Mansell Collection **18** top, **20**, **26** top, **48** right, **51** top right; Popperfoto **9**, **31** right, **35** top left and top right, **37** bottom left, **47** left, **53**, **54** top, **55** bottom right, **56** top and bottom, **60** bottom right, **61** top, **68** top, **78** right, **80** left and right; Radio Times Hulton Picture Library front endpapers, **4/5**, **11** right, **12**, **15** bottom, **17** bottom, **18** bottom left, **19** top and bottom, **21** top and bottom, **22** top right and bottom, **26** centre left, bottom left and bottom right, **30** top and bottom left, **48** left, **58** top right, **64** top and bottom, **65** left, **76** left, **77** bottom left; Sport and General Press Agency **34** bottom left, **62** top; Syndication International **24** bottom, **29** bottom left, **32** top right, **33** top right and bottom right, **40**, **41** top right and bottom, **42** top left, **47** right, **50** left, **51** top left, **59** right, **60** bottom left, **62** bottom, **63** left, **66** top, **72** right, **77** top right; The Times **29** top, **72** left.

Jacket and cover

Camera Press inset right front; Colorsport left front; Le-Roye Productions right front and back; Syndication International inset left front.

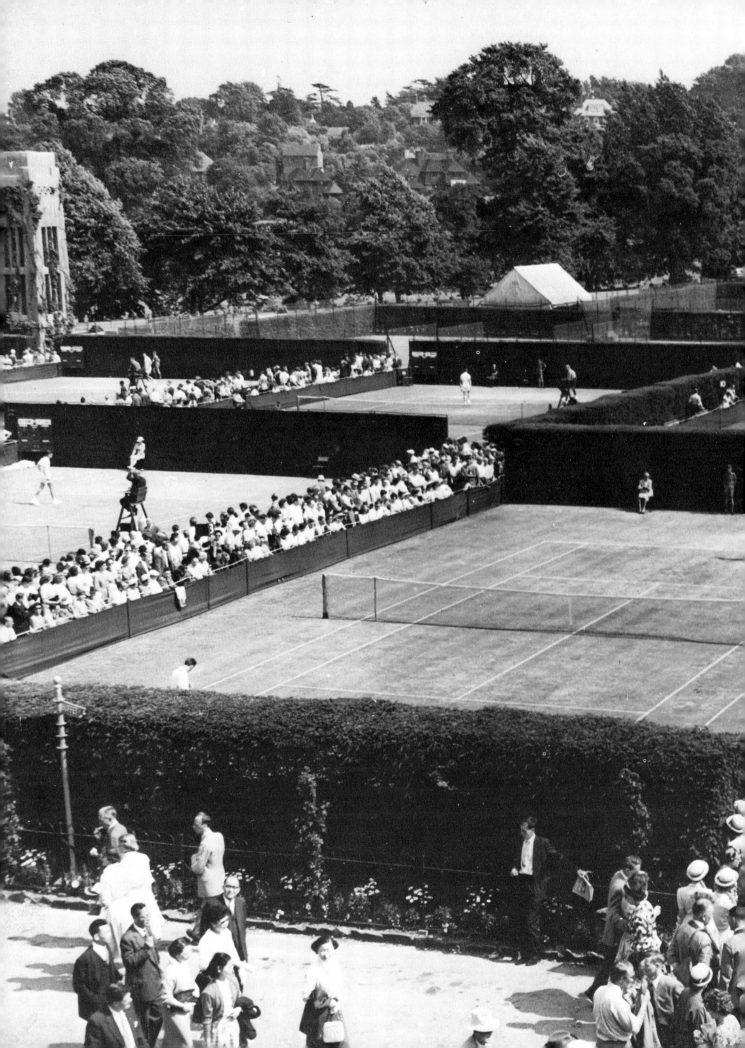